The Peaceful Season

Rev. Roger A. Swenson

The Peaceful Season

Daily Advent Meditations for Everyday Christians

ALBA · HOUSE   NEW · YORK

SOCIETY OF ST. PAUL, 2187 VICTORY BLVD., STATEN ISLAND, NEW YORK 10314

Library of Congress Cataloging in Publication Data

Swenson, Roger A.
  The peaceful season.

  Bibliography: p.
  1. Advent — Meditations.   I. Title.
BV40.S93   1987   242'.33   87-1047
ISBN 0-8189-0519-0

Nihil Obstat:
Rev. Mons. Henry C. Bezou
Censor Librorum

Imprimatur:
Most Rev. Philip M. Hannan
Archbishop of New Orleans
January 20, 1987

Designed, printed and bound in the United States of
America by the Fathers and Brothers of the
Society of St. Paul, 2187 Victory Boulevard,
Staten Island, New York 10314, as part of their
communications apostolate.

---

1 2 3 4 5 6 7 8 9 (Current Printing: first digit)

---

to

Charles Torpey, Jr.

FOREWORD

You are about to begin a restful journey toward a meaningful Christmas celebration. *The Peaceful Season* is a "thought for the day" approach to prayer set to modern times with theological precision. Using the daily liturgical texts of Advent, one single idea is expressed with concise clarity, harmonized by imaginatively lilting poetry, concluding with an original prayer.

Father Swenson possesses keen insight into human nature and pastoral practice, a masterful ability at spiritual psychology and a refreshingly reflective grasp of Sacred Scripture.

For the busy lay person, for the frenzied priest or religious, for the neophyte or veteran at private prayer, this little volume asks for only a quarter hour with the Lord each day. I predict that those fifteen minutes with these thoughtful promptings will enliven your day and your Advent. To await Christmas with *The Peaceful Season* is to insure yourself a spiritual and devotional means of making sense out of all that has trafficked upon this sacred season in secular society and perhaps in your own life.

Treat yourself to an uplifting Advent. You will be more grateful about the Lord's coming and equally indebted to Father Swenson for helping to make that possible. Enjoy this Advent gift.

† MOST REV. JOHN C. FAVALORA
Bishop of Alexandria

INTRODUCTION

We live in a kingdom of now and not yet. In no season is the tension generated by this paradox felt more acutely than in Advent. The now sparkles beguilingly from the tinseled trees and winking lights. We are urged to indulge ourselves now, to fulfill our friends' wishes now, to make real our children's dreams now. The first Christmas commercial startled us when it appeared on television in mid-October. It was silly, we thought, to be so premature. Then, suddenly, came the deluge. By Thanksgiving we were caught in the undertow, pulled from our moorings, drawn by the siren song of publicity to far distant shores, finding ourselves shipwrecked on the shoals of a different shopping mall each week. And that was merely prelude to December's rhapsody, that fugue of gift and counter-gift which plays in our dreams each night and makes us sit up straight in bed to recall Aunt Fran's favorite color.

So much money, so much time and energy and snake oil is expended to convince us that Christmas is now. The Christmas spirit dictates generosity now. Greetings must be heartier now. Salespersons must be kinder now. Bargains must be more outrageous now.

The Christian wonders about all this. Like everyone else, the Christian scurries to stores and worries over menus, but in those all too rare moments of truth — the wait at the railroad crossing, the walk to class, the unwinding before sleep — the Christian comes up against the well-hidden reality: December 3rd isn't Christmas. Neither is the 15th or the 21st. Christmas is not yet.

This book of meditations is written for all of you who can stand the not yet, who can snatch fifteen or twenty minutes from each Advent day to prepare for the coming of the Prince of Peace. The insights offered here are based on the daily and Sunday Scripture readings found in the Masses of the season. Whether they are drawn from the Old or the New Testament, the passages which begin each meditation are obviously not part of the Christmas ritual. The Church teaches the lessons of Advent as the Old Testament readings reveal the hopes of a people yearning for a Messiah and the Gospel passages present the proximate preparation for One who will be more than a savior of a people, more than the redeemer of any one nation.

This book is about waiting, yearning, purification: the necessary work of preparation. It is about Christmas only to the extent that the holy day will not come without a season of hope to herald it. This book is about how humankind's longing to greet the newborn Son of God has been encapsulated by the Church into approximately four weeks of active, productive anticipation.

Above all, this book is about peace. In these meditations, you will discover how to position yourself for the coming of the Prince of Peace by practicing peace each day. You will be led, if you so allow yourself, to find serenity in struggle, tranquility in turmoil, silent joy as you joust with the world. From time to time, the Holy Spirit will bless you with one or another of his seven gifts, sweet yet sturdy charisms to steel you and soothe you as now and not yet seem to pull you apart.

This peace in the midst of a month of distractions will require an earnest payment, a token of your commitment best summed up in Pascal's succinct reminder:

> All the troubles of life come upon us because we refuse to sit quietly for a while each day in our rooms.

You must find a prayer place — your room, your basement, your garage, your church — where the sounds of the season are blotted out. No premature Christmas songs or pitchmen's cries shall penetrate this retreat. Make no mistake, you will pay a price for spending fifteen or twenty minutes in such solitude. Many will find this price quite high: some things won't get done, some people won't be able to find you. The important thing is that God will be able to find you and you will be able to find him. If you have trouble taking the time and making the place, imagine what your day would be like without this quiet haven.

Peace will come to you in this place, that peace which is the blending of the now and the not yet. Christ was born two thousand years ago; he is still here for you whenever you turn to him. He is here for you now. But he is not yet yours as long as your life is filled with the commercial clutter of this December. If you cannot step aside with him, then you will not know his presence; you will not know his "now" in your "not yet."

The season of Advent recapitulates the history of the world before the birth of Christ. Men and women of every race and nation longed to see God smile. Their ways were primitive, their dreams outlandish. But their hope was sincere, and their prayers were answered. Most of us can find an accurate reflection of our lives in the topography of Advent. Peaks of assurance compete with valleys of doubt in a land of possibility. We, too, long to see God smile. We believe he loves us now. We are confident in his forgiveness now. We rejoice at his Eucharistic banquet now. But because of our faulty memory and our selective attention, we often feel that we have not yet seen him smile. Advent prepares us for that smile, reminds us that we have seen it before, and, if we allow the holy season to have its way, invites us to pronounce our own benediction. You can't really say "peace" without smiling.

> Insignificant man, escape from your everyday business for a short while, hide for a moment from your restless thoughts. Break off from your cares and troubles and be less concerned about your tasks and labors. Make a little time for God and rest a while in him.
>
> Enter into your mind's inner chamber. Shut out everything but God and whatever helps you to seek him; and when you have shut the door, look for him. Speak now to God and say with your whole heart: *I seek your face; your face, Lord, I desire.*
>
> St. Anselm

I am grateful to Father Anthony Chenevey, S.S.P., Editor-in-Chief of Alba House Publications, for his assistance in this and other endeavors. His kindness and patience will remain among the most pleasant of the memories which flow from the composition of this work.

R.A.S

Daily Advent Meditations
for Everyday Christians

FIRST SUNDAY OF ADVENT

Jesus said, "Look around you! You do not know when the master of the house is coming, whether at dusk, at midnight, when the cock crows, or at early dawn. Do not let him come suddenly and catch you asleep. What I say to you, I say to all: Be on guard!" (Mk 13:35-37).

The Church's year has turned. The flowering of the spirit is long since ended. Autumn intervened splashing the landscape of the soul with bright colors; orange and crimson flames curled and fell. They lie now a brittle coverlet on the heart. Too late and too little, the wan sun barely makes a day. Good Christians wonder weakly what the new year will bring.

The peace of Advent is hard-won. So much of the world begins its frenzy of preparation for Christmas. While the spirit rests uneasily, beset with memories of communions past, the business of December accelerates. Each day, each week brings us closer to being too late. Advent has become schizoid. The deep peace that should be part of our preparation is shattered by a holiday that begins weeks too soon.

It takes strength to separate Advent from Christmas, a deliberate decision to let the soul lie fallow for four weeks in order that God may do his work. Advent should be a night time, a period of silence when one's hearing becomes attuned to the footsteps of the Master. "Whether at dusk, at midnight, when the cock crows, or at early dawn," the Master will return. "Be on guard" lest he find your souls asleep,

lulled into unprotesting deafness by the white noise of commerce. The Advent vocation is not simply to stay awake, but
to be alert to the silent footfall, the whispered invitation.
The Father's desire is that we celebrate the birth of his Son
on the day appointed. The Father's regret is our hyperactiv-
ity in these weeks, this continual pseudo-celebration of that
which is not yet ours to embrace. As the Christ Child waits in
his mother's womb, so must we rest in quiet hope.

Hope is our Advent virtue, hope that the fallow fields
will again bloom, hope that each sleeping bud will be trans-
formed, hope that a new year will bring new faith and
fervor. But, today, hope is fragile and frightened. It burrows
deeper beneath the coverlet as our lives overflow with the
sounds of the season. Christmas will not come without a
season of hope to herald it. Hope is our Advent virtue. Peace
is hope's reward.

Advent, like Lent, is a time of preparation, and preparation calls for resolution. On this first day of the Church's
new year, resolve to nurture the ambience of peace, that
attitude of watchful waiting of which Isaiah speaks: "Would
that you might meet us doing right, that we were mindful of
you in our ways!" (Is 64:4). Lying fallow does not mean lying
dead. This is a season to be mindful of the Lord and of the
many ways in which he reveals himself to you. Nurture the
seeds of silence within. In the silence of this season, God will
speak to you. Shun the brightness without. In the darkness
of this season, God will show himself to you. Seek the silence
and the darkness of prayer for there waits the God of
Advent.

> Dusk, the haze of day's end
> makes a fool of vision,
> turns betrayed perception
> inward to the Light.

Midnight seals the bargain,
double locks the senses.
Now the Master's footsteps
concentrate the mind.

Cock crow comes by instinct,
marks a world just turning
while the heart beats slowly
sounding deep His peace.

Dawn, another season
brings the threat of frenzy.
Still the heart in darkness
listens for His call.

Come, Lord Jesus, to the place I have made for you, a place of quiet trust, serene faith, and peaceful anticipation. Or is this the place you have made for me? Thank you, Lord Jesus.   Amen.

MONDAY OF THE FIRST WEEK

Jesus showed amazement on hearing this and remarked
to his followers, "I assure you, I have never found this much
faith in Israel" (Mt 8:10).

The peace which the season of Advent should bring to hearts can be only as deep as faith will permit. To seek peace without a foundation of faith in the Lord is to chase the elusive butterfly. This necessary dependence of peace on faith saddens and discourages many because they believe their faith is weak. The beginning of this season of peace is an appropriate time to take a faith inventory. Chances are good that you will find that your faith measures up, that you do possess the foundation upon which inner peace can rest.

Creedal faith is not the issue here. The faith which you profess in church each week is bare-bones belief. All good Christians believe in God, the creator and lawgiver; Christ, the healer and redeemer; the Holy Spirit of truth and discernment. According to his or her own interpretation, the good Christian believes in the holy, catholic church. But such statements, no matter how fervently recited, are dry as dust when applied to a situation of inner turmoil. Except for those martyrs who died ostensibly for a point of dogma, no one can take much comfort from the fact that Jesus is begotten, not made, one in being with the Father. The faith which underlies peace of soul is not merely recited, but experienced.

Does your faith inventory include compassion? Although the patient was but a serving boy, the centurion in today's Gospel was deeply distraught over his illness. Humility? The Roman turned to a Jew for help, perhaps his last resort. Does your faith inventory include submission to authority? The centurion, a non-commissioned officer, knew what it meant to command and to obey. Does your faith have a voice? Do you tell God what you need? The centurion stated his case boldly. Is your faith content to trust the Lord to work in his own way? "Just give an order," said the centurion. These are some of the marks of a living faith, the kind of faith upon which true peace can rest: Compassion. Humility. Submissiveness. Prayer. Trust. Taken another way, inner peace cannot rest upon the sharp thrusts of egocentricity, arrogance, exaggerated individualism, or skepticism. Many in our society practice the art of peacemaking as if they lived in a vacuum. To them, peace is a delicate construct within, which must be laboriously assembled and ferociously protected against forces from without. Instead, lasting inner peace relies on faith in God, faith in neighbor, faith in self.

Today, survey the characteristics of your faith. If inner peace eludes you, the cause probably lies in your relationship with another, the Other, or yourself. Think of the peace which the centurion must have experienced even before he arrived home to find his beloved serving boy on the mend. That peace rested upon a faith which prompted him to care for another, to seek aid without prejudice, to bow to authority, to ask a favor, to allow for a better way. Compassion + Humility + Submissiveness + Prayer + Trust = Faith. If you seek peace, strive to balance this equation.

> I built a castle for my peace
> protected it with sword and spear
> then filled the moat with cold disdain
> to keep the world from coming near.
>
> They clamored at the battlements
> for rift and chink sought high and low
> expecting once inside to share
> the treasure I was yet to know.
>
> From room to thick-walled room I fled
> the muffled sounds of envy's cry
> in search of one calm silent spot
> in which to breathe a grateful sigh.
>
> Through countless chambers did I seek
> that soundless pure unpeopled place
> until the final door revealed
> a mirrored den and my own face.
>
> I built a fortress of distrust
> locked out the prattle of the crowd.
> Now all I hear is in my room
> self-mockery that laughs aloud.

Lord Jesus, send your Holy Spirit upon us. Strengthen our faith in the goodness of your heavenly Father, unite us in the bond of mutual trust, and make of us a firm foundation for the house of peace. Amen.

TUESDAY OF THE FIRST WEEK

The spirit of the Lord shall rest upon him:
    a spirit of wisdom and understanding,
A spirit of counsel and strength,
    a spirit of knowledge and fear of the Lord,
    and his delight shall be fear of the Lord (Is 11:2-3).

The idea that the indwelling of the Holy Spirit brings to the soul seven special gifts is based in part on this passage from Isaiah. (For the first mention of *fear of the Lord*, other translations and the Church's tradition have substituted *piety*.) We might call these charisms seven "pre-Christmas" presents, the gifts of Advent. They are requisites for the task of discernment which is the necessary prelude to the true peace of this season. One might suppose these gifts are too grand for the simple quest for peace; the truth is that they are very down-to-earth. These pre-Christmas presents from the Lord help us to conform our wills to his will. From time to time in these pages, we shall meditate on each of the seven gifts of the Holy Spirit and their application to our daily lives, especially that part of our life we call Advent. Today, wisdom.

Of all the foggy words that have entered the lexicon in recent times, the oddest must be *prioritization*. Besides being quite ungainly, it makes trivial the honest act of setting priorities, a valid strategy, born in the armed services, perfected in the business community, and now adopted by religious and psychological counselors. Setting priorities can hasten spiritual healing and lead to the restoration of emotional balance. The gift of the Holy Spirit called wisdom is the gift of setting priorities.

Spiritual wisdom is nothing less than the knowledge of God. It is immediately evident that, as with all the gifts of the Spirit, wisdom is possessed in degrees. How many of us can claim to know God? We may have an insight here and a glimpse there, a good hour of prayer in which we were joyously lifted up, a sweet moment of consolation in time of trial. But, in truth, we do not so much know God as we know things about him. Yet, that is quite enough to allow the gift of wisdom to operate in us, quite enough to set wise priorities.

What we know about God is primarily this: he is our Guide and our Goal. We were made to live with him forever. That was his doing. Our lives are guided toward that everlasting happiness. That is his doing. Now, if God is our Guide and our Goal, wisdom tells us how to order our priorities so that we may conform ourselves to his guidance and arrive at our goal. Wisdom is the old man at the side of the road who tells the directionless slicker with the big car, "Nope, I don't know how far it is to Central City. Don't know the way to the four-lane. Don't know how to get to Titusville." When the exasperated traveler explodes with, "You don't know much, do you?" the old man says, "Nope, but I ain't lost."

Wisdom is never lost. While it isn't a roadmap to heaven or a sneak preview of the Beatific Vision, it does help us to get our directions straight. Most of us lack a grand scheme for salvation; we count ourselves lucky if we can make plans for one day. That's where this very practical gift of the Holy Spirit comes in. Unless you are an international jewel thief, you know pretty well what today will be like, what barriers will have to be hurdled, what challenges will confront you. Wisdom helps you order your decisions based on your ultimate Goal. Wisdom is part of the guidance system that God sends you, an inner sense of priority that reveals what is wheat and what is chaff. Today, apply the Spirit's gift of wisdom to your decisions. Among the valuable effects of this very practical application is the blessing of peace. Peace is part of pointing yourself toward God.

Cast off the lines,
this ship would sail
upon the wild and rolling tide
to haven calm
beyond the bar
that separates the sun from night.

These cables prove
too stout to bend,
so petrified with barnacles
that they refuse
to give her room
to turn her prow to distant shores.

Apply the ax
to strings attached
to goods and deals and triumphs mean,
the halter of
an anchored world
which keeps this soul detained in port.

Let go the lines,
this ship would turn
to that safe harbor 'neath the Light
which shines to guide
all those to peace
who seek direction in the storm.

Lord, our Goal and Guide, send your Holy Spirit of wisdom upon us who sail this stormy sea. Keep before us always the pole star of your love, that we may wisely measure the glitter of this world against it.   Amen.

WEDNESDAY OF THE FIRST WEEK

The Lord is my shepherd; I shall not want.
In verdant pastures he gives me repose;
Beside restful waters he leads me;
he refreshes my soul (Ps 23:1-2).

What is it about today's Responsorial Psalm that makes it the favorite of so many? It seems so foreign to the mass culture of industrial society. In an age when half the people of the Western world live in great cities, how can a pastoral vision of flocks and pastures and restful waters have any relevance to the slam-bang world of instant communication and deadline dementia? Nostalgia, at least in the common usage of the word, can have little to do with this attraction to shepherds' staffs and anointed heads. Very few of us were brought up in such bucolic surroundings. We can't actually remember being part of a picture such as the psalmist paints. Perhaps we've enjoyed a similar scene on a Public Television show featuring lost cultures, but the attraction of this psalm is stronger than the brief allure of a media presentation.

For Christians who read the Bible, there is another kind of nostalgia, not a remembrance of things past, but a yearning for things as they might have been had not mankind mucked things up. Psalm 23 in an exercise in innocence. It appeals to all of us saddened by our loss of innocence. You and I have made parking lots of verdant pastures. We have caused restful waters to bubble and foam with pollutants. The table once spread before us is now the plastic-topped counter of a fast food chain. Our souls are chock-a-block with interest rates and power plays and soap operas. We are filled with regret for the mess we've made of things. No wonder just a few words about refreshment give rise to an almost unbearable yearning for what might have been. That desire, however, is quickly reined in by the reality and practicality of the daily grind.

Advent is a time to release this special yearning from the shackles of producing, achieving, and winning, a time to give free rein to this nostalgia for what might have been. As the death of winter approaches, a last hurrah is in order. This is a day to let your soul seek its own level, a day to pull out a piece of paper and make a list of where you would like to be and what you would like to do. See God, today, as giving you permission to indulge your fancy and describe your paradise.

At first, your Eden may take on the familiar characteristics of the everyday scenery that jabs you in the ribs and scrapes your shins. All you want is a bit more pay or prestige, the healing of a specific relationship, a better method of prayer. As your soul, with God's permission, heads for its own territory, a gradual transformation will occur. Little by little, the specifics of immediate gratification fade away; you find yourself in a scene much like the psalmist described. It is a place you have never seen before; there are no comfortable points of reference. Your soul becomes simple. The crack and crush of commerce and home-making and child-rearing recede into the background. Instead of what you thought you wanted and needed — the task accomplished, the strategy finessed — you have unaccountably discovered a place of peace in your living room or the parish church.

God has drawn your city soul to a pasture with a stream running through it. He has invited you to lie down on the green grass and dangle your hand in the cool water. You have never been here before but you know it must be home.

Now you sense that the shepherd is just over that crocus-covered knoll, that he is about to appear as he makes his way to you. But you must return. You will just miss him as you go back to the moil of men, but this time refreshed, this time with enduring peace. Your hand tingles with the remembrance of the cool water, that nostalgia for what might have been, and is.

> Sleep, my soul,
> and dream a past that never was.
> Let peace flow through your reveries,
> a stream refreshing and refreshed
> by shepherd's song of what will be
> become what is. And rest in hope.
> Accept the sweet surprise that Peace
> dreams of you.

Shepherd of souls, lead me to a land of sweet repose where I may recline at your side unmoved by the world's contentions. Let me know enduring peace and, at the appointed hour, carry it back to my troubled sisters and brothers.   Amen.

THURSDAY OF THE FIRST WEEK

Jesus said, "Anyone who hears my words and puts them into practice is like the wise man who built his house on rock. When the rainy season set in, the torrents came and the winds blew and buffeted his house. It did not collapse; it had been set on rock" (Mt 7:24-25).

Only in California? There on the television screen was a luxurious home sliding down a rain-soaked hill toward the Pacific. The newscaster gave assurance that it wasn't supposed to be this way while the camera obligingly focussed on the hill above which had collapsed after three days of torrential rain. The final comment from the owner to the reporter was just succinct enough to fit the medium's message. Looking down at his home as the sea welcomed it, he said, "I never thought it would happen to me."

That was a statement of belief. Building on the spongy hill was an act of faith, faith that fate would look elsewhere for a victim, faith founded on a life of good fortune up to now. Knowledge might also have been involved. Perhaps the owner tested the earth before he built. Perhaps he drove the pilings extra deep. He might have even hired an engineer who assured him that modern construction methods would prevent any calamity. He probably slept quite peacefully at night with all that faith and knowledge. Until the last night. When the house started to move, he knew that faith and knowledge didn't guarantee peaceful sleep. Something more was needed.

The news item supported none of this kind of speculation. But I wonder if the owner of that runaway house would have been meat for the media had he taken certain steps during the rainy season, like testing the porosity of the earth each day, or measuring the height of the pilings to see if they were sinking, or something simpler like rolling a ball across the kitchen floor to see if it came to rest or bounced out the door. There must have been certain actions, daily tests, to prevent the need for this middle of the night flight to safety.

Whether or not Advent is a rainy season where you live, it is wise to seek a solid foundation for the peace you deserve. Jesus tells us in today's Gospel that faith and knowledge by themselves will not support true and lasting peace. Another ingredient is needed: the solidity of action. Those who cry out, "Lord, Lord," may know who the Master is. They may believe in his power to save, but unless they embrace the habit of acting on this faith and knowledge, the substructure can give way. The man with the wayward house was knowledgeable and trusted the experts, but he took no action when action was called for. His peace was as impermanent as the foundation of his home.

You would not be reading this book if you had not the faith of a Christian and the knowledge which comes with being a student of the spirit. The peace of this season or of any season requires one thing more: your faith must be made manifest in action; your knowledge must bear fruit in Christian witness. Only if you get out of your spiritual house and look around will you see what needs to be done. Advent is a time of peace, to be sure, but peace is another word for the satisfaction that is yours in making the Christian message come to life in your daily encounter with the world.

If the peace of this season eludes you, look around your spiritual home. You will find many things which need to be done, many wrongs to be made right, many people who are hurting, many bruised relationships to be reconciled. These are all signs that your house could begin to creak and tip and slide away. Reinforce your faith, buttress your knowledge, base your hope for peace solidly on the rock of Christian witness. "Lord, Lord" isn't enough. Peace says, "Send me."

> Make straight for the heart of the matter.
> Let nothing deter your intention
> to savor the peace that is offered
> in your quiet dreamland of Eden.

Though chains of affliction around you
may hobble the steps of your conscience,
do not slow your pace when approaching
this haven to which you seek entrance.

Fly swiftly past soulful entreaties,
past envy at your resolution,
the clutch of the hand that would keep you
from tasting the sweetness of languor.

But know, in this flight through affliction,
the distance from here to safe harbor
is doubled each time that you race by
one shackled to stock-still misfortune.

Father of the afflicted, you sent your Son to bring peace to those broken on the rack of the world. Let me join them in humble compassion so that I may know both the gift and the Giver.   Amen.

FEAST OF THE
IMMACULATE CONCEPTION*

"The Holy Spirit will come upon you and the power of the Most High will overshadow you; hence, the holy offspring to be born will be called Son of God. Know that Elizabeth your kinswoman has conceived a son in her old age; she who was thought to be sterile is now in her sixth month, for nothing is impossible with God" (Lk 1:35-37)

---

* Friday of the first week of Advent is the earliest day on which the Feast of the Immaculate Conception can be celebrated. Substitute this meditation for that provided for the day on which December 8th falls.

She was an easy mark, almost begging to be ripped off with that shopping bag full-up with bright little packages. He had spotted her on the subway, alerted by her stooped shoulders and senior shuffle. He went out the other door first so he could watch her get off. She wasn't as old as he liked them, but one look at her lips clinched the deal. They moved in that familiar one-sided conversation carried on by the old ones when they are scared stiff. He liked them scared, paralyzed scared. When they were rigid, they didn't fight back. They just held on brittle until you broke the hold.

It was too easy. When he got to street level, he crossed and kept ahead of her. Two streets down, she turned into Third. He went up a block and down the alley and waited in a doorway. The only thing that worried him as she approached on the shadowed, nearly empty sidewalk was that she kept her right hand, the one not holding her purchases, in the open purse suspended by its strap from her shoulder. Did she have a gun in there? He hesitated. Now she got close enough so he could again see her lips moving. "Senile," he thought, "no gun on this granny." He snapped open his knife and wondered what she had in her right hand.

It just took a second. The shopping bag almost jumped into his arms as he broke the handle. He knocked her down with one blow, cut the strap on the purse and took it off her hand to reveal a tightly-clutched rosary. As she sat on the cold sidewalk, her lips still moved silently. The rosary was silver and crystal, good for a couple of bucks, or maybe Tanya would like it. He had time, so he pulled it hard. She resisted with some strength and started to get up.

"Don't take my tears," she pleaded. He had to hit her twice, hard and angry across the face, and actually step on her wrist to loosen her grip. He walked away, not fast, not slow, like always. She was crying like they all do. Just before he turned the corner, he heard her whimper, "Not my tears."

Tanya didn't want it. She said it was a sin to wear it around your neck and she didn't know the prayers. She thought her Gramma might like it, so they took it to the old woman who poured the beads from hand to hand and thanked him for Mary's tears.

"Mary's tears, what's that?"

"When you pray these beads, you are counting the tears of the Holy Virgin. She had so many sorrows. Her parents were too old to play with her. She was kept locked up away from men, a virgin girl. In the Temple, her heart was pierced with a sword and Jesus turned his back on her. She followed him and saw how people hated him. All the tears she cried are on these beads. When Jesus died, she was there, and when he was buried, and when her husband died. All those tears, and chased by a dragon."

He was impressed, listening, not so tough right now, but Tanya just winked. He thought of his mother, or tried to, she was so long gone.

"And the Holy Virgin cries with *you* when things go bad. These beads are yours as much as hers. I used to pray, Tan-Tan. Every day I used to pray before I got sick for your Grampa and your Aunt Paula and my poor Jimmy with his polio. Every time I touched a bead, I knew it was another one of Blessed Mary's tears. Her tears are so powerful they can make Jesus cry. Jesus will do whatever she says. He can't stand to see his mother cry. Jesus saved Jimmy because his mother cried. And your Aunt Paula and your Grampa are in heaven because the Holy Virgin cried to Jesus when I touched the beads."

The old lady seemed to doze off but still held so tightly to her gift that Tanya couldn't pry her fingers apart. He remembered those other knobby hands this afternoon and heard again the weak cry.

He was not surprised the next day when the stuff in the shopping bag didn't bring much — poor little presents. Cheap junk for her hard-up neighbors, he guessed. Still, he got nearly ten dollars for the whole lot. Five more of his own and the forty-three cents from the purse covered his purchase at the religious goods store. He went back to the subway, determined to wait as long as it took.

A rose arises from the earth,
a miracle beheld
by all who tread the frozen land
to come just near
enough to drink
her fragrance mild
and gaze upon
the fragile bud
and thornless stem.

Now shy, they back away for fear
of sullying with rough
impertinence this winter bloom,
perfection in
the midst of soiled
exhausted stares,
this hope conceived
when hope was lost,
this thrust to God.

Not seen but sensed the vital grace,
which wafts from petals charged
with mystery immaculate,
reveals the love
hid deep within
the root pristine,
the tendril pure,
protected by
the hand of God.

They stand away, perplexed by doubt
that such a flower could live
in this impure forbidding clime,
sore tempted to
pull from the soil
bud stem and root
to prove a hoax
on hope, and yet
they stand away.

Virgin of all virgins blest, intercede for us and our skeptical world.
Ask of your holy Son the grace we need to bring to the bereaved
consolation, to the separated unity, to the anxious peace, to the
sinner forgiveness, to the impossible dreamers the possibility of
fulfillment. Amen.

FRIDAY OF THE FIRST WEEK

For the tyrant will be no more
　　and the arrogant will have gone;
All who are alert to do evil will be cut off,
　　those whose mere word condemns a man,
Who ensnare his defender at the gate,
　　and leave the just man with an empty claim (Is 29:20-21).

Tyranny is out of fashion, so foreign to contemporary Western culture that most would be hard put even to imagine life under the heel of an arbitrary and absolute ruler. This is not to say that tyranny is dead; it flourishes to this day in countries and kingdoms whose names appear briefly in the newspapers. Most Americans would describe tyranny in doctrinaire terms. Tyranny means oppression of the many by the few. The many are subjected, exploited, degraded. The few are merciless, inflexible, vindictive. When we think of tyranny at all, we view it from afar, shudder at the absolutism, and give thanks that we live in freedom. It is quite understandable that Isaiah's dream of the day tyranny ends in Israel seems archaic to us. The coming of the Messiah, for which we prepare in Advent, will bring about the realization of many hopes in our hearts. The end of tyranny is not one of them.

It comes as a shock, then, to learn that Isaiah's dream is as valid today as it was 2700 years ago. Each of us has at least one tyrant in our lives. The tyrant is the perverse habit, the propensity to choose darkness rather than light. There are few things more dispiriting in the quest for the peaceful heart than to feel the familiar tug of a habit you thought you had conquered. In a moment, by the slimmest thread of forgotten pleasure, hard-won progress toward the balanced life is pulled to a grinding halt. The peaceful season becomes a season of regret. The tyrant's iron boot is back on your neck. The air is thick with self-accusation. Could there be a more humbling admission? "I can *not* control myself."

One of the best reasons for carving out a little slice of peace each Advent day is that it affords time for strategic planning. Strategy is the most powerful weapon against the tyrant because strategy is a luxury of the foresighted and every habitual failure requires lead time. Habit sees you coming and sets you up. Strategy allows you to turn the tables. Strategy lets you see habit from afar and gives you time to take evasive action.

Concentrate today on one of the habits you would most like to out-maneuver. See it for what it is, a tyrant which you have allowed to wrest from you control of your life. Describe the tyrant. What time does he usually attack? From now until then is the time you have to arm yourself. Whom does he travel with? These are the people for whom you have to set a nightwatch. Where are you when the sirens sound? What are you usually doing? All these details and more are necessary for your strategy. When you name the aggressor, describe him, plot his course, you are taking over. You are regaining control over your life.

When you are ready to develop your strategy, it will seem very obvious. Habit-breaking strategy is based on two maneuvers: substitution and removal. Remember, you have identified the tyrant. You know his course and his timing. You can remove either the temptation or yourself from the field of battle. Or when the attack begins, you can choose to do something better. Occupy yourself with something you can control rather than giving in to something you can't. The key to either method is to use the extra time which Advent gives you to look ahead, to plan how to out-general the tyrant.

No habit which offends God can ever be conquered without prayer. It's only reasonable to ask God for the strength necessary to live a life which pleases him. Pray in your quiet time when you make your plans to outflank the tyrant. Pray during the day as your mind races ahead to the battle. Above all, pray at the moment the tyrant's forces are upon you. God gives his power to those who ask. Plan, pray, and ask.

Death to all tyrants,
cry the reformers,
toppling the statues,
wielding the axes.

While the drip
        drip
           drip
     on the flagstone
     'neath the rainspout
and the chip
        chip
          chip
     on the redwood
     by the termite
bring
   us
       down
          finally
splitting like rocks in an earthquake,
falling like trees in the forest.

Sing out the anthem,
soldiers of heaven!
How can a man hear
dripping and chipping?

---

*Spirit of Wisdom, we ask not to see the future, but simply to see
ahead. Bathe our worldly eyes with your saving grace so that we may
perceive in time the dangers which lie in our path. Guide us past the
snares.   Amen.*

SATURDAY OF THE FIRST WEEK

O people of Zion, who dwell in Jerusalem,
  no more will you weep;
He will be gracious to you when you cry out,
  as soon as he hears he will answer you (Is 30:19).

Forewarned is forearmed. Even a brief examination of the ways we have fallen in the past will provide valuable strategies for defeating our perverse habits. But strategies aren't enough. Good intentions are not enough. If we are going to succeed in preparing our hearts to be fit dwelling places for the Prince of Peace, we must give ourselves to the refiner's fire. If we would be victorious over evil, the confrontation must occur. With Jesus we say,"I have come to light a fire on the earth. How I wish the blaze were ignited" (Lk 12:49). This is not to say that we go looking for evil in order to test our strategy. That is not necessary. Evil will search us out. But when evil does find us, the meeting must be that of two adversaries. We encounter evil almost every hour of every day. We usually pass by like a ship in a fog avoiding the barrier reef, wary of proximity. We are good Christians and devote more than a modicum of energy and common sense to remaining so.

We do not, however, steam past our habits of sin with such equanimity. Here we have been too often crushed on the rocks. We remain quite alert in the presence of this familiar evil, armed as we are with our strategies and good intentions. This is one meeting which must take place; not a brief encounter, it must be a confrontation, a fight with one winner. Yet, despite the plans, the intentions, the fortitude, we lose. Why? Because we want to lose.

We want to give in. Something goes awry in our interior compass and tells us that for this moment this evil disguised as good is more valuable than anything else, more valuable than self-respect, more valuable than heaven itself. Pretending to believe this lie to be the highest truth, we forgo the ultimate weapon in our arsenal. We choose not to call upon the power of God. Knowing that his power is infinitely greater than any evil, we refuse to ask for it, for to do so would guarantee the loss of the greatest of goods (evil disguised) we could dream of. We swallow the one prayer which would decisively tilt the scales of battle: "God help me!" We lose again.

With all the foreknowledge, strategy, good intentions, and thirst for the fight which common sense and the Holy Spirit offer, we are conquered again by perverse habit because we choose to believe a lie. A momentary act which we know to be harmful to our physical, psychological, or spiritual health is presented to us as that one great good for this time and this place, and perhaps for all times and all places. We know it's a lie. All logic points to its absurdity. But we choose to believe because to do otherwise would deprive us of the pleasure of the moment, not to mention involving us in a moral struggle in which God would have to be invoked and a winner declared. "Too much," we cry. "I know it's a lie; the simplest thing is to believe that this evil is really good." The losses mount; our resistance weakens; a habit becomes a way of life.

The peace of this season will not come to those who are the slaves of unhealthy habits, for this kind of habit is built on the lie that evil is good. Peace and untruth cannot coexist. The Prince of Peace and the Way, the Truth, and the Life are one and the same person. Use the moments of silence which you have wrenched from the world during these December days to identify and isolate the habits that play you false. Devise a strategy to defeat them. Don't rely on your good will. Don't believe for a moment that the diamond seeming to reflect in its facets all your dreams is anything but paste. Then call on the power of victory: "God help me!" You know he will answer you as soon as he hears you.

Close the gate	the horse is gone
Seek the peace	the war's begun
Check the gas	the car has stopped
Spring the trap	the rabbit's run
Don the mac	the cold is caught
Speak the truth	the lie has won
Cheer the team	the game is lost
Pray the Lord	the evil's done

Lord of power and might, in fear of my own lack of fortitude, I call upon you now before the battle. Give me strength and wisdom when my adversary appears so that I might speak your name on the field of conflict as easily as I do in this place of peace.   Amen.

SECOND SUNDAY OF ADVENT

A voice cries out:
In the desert prepare the way of the Lord!
    Make straight in the wasteland a highway for our God!
Every valley shall be filled in,
    every mountain and hill shall be made low;
The rugged land shall be made a plain,
    the rough country a broad valley (Is 40:3-4).

The Advent pilgrim seeks a straight path through the distractions of the season. At first, it seems that a desert experience is required. "In the desert prepare the way of the Lord!" A weekend retreat, perhaps, a few hours of solitude

— the calm, fruitful emptiness of being alone with the Lord. Unfortunately, most of us are bound to the frenzy of our world by steel strands of duty. In a way, this inability to escape the world is a blessing, for the Prince of Peace was sent not only to a few hermits but also to millions of frazzled commuters and hassled homemakers. We must learn to find the peace of Christ here amid the din.

The second of the seven gifts of the Holy Spirit, those pre-Christmas presents of Advent, is understanding. Spiritual understanding is our guide when we seek a straight path in the wasteland. No matter how rough our daily road, understanding is the lamp which illuminates heaven's gate, the beacon which draws us forward to eternal life. Understanding reminds us that what we see around us will pass away. Understanding burnishes those gifts which last and highlights the sterility of those glories which fade.

In your quiet quarter-hour today, let the lamp of understanding bathe the landscape of your life. Remember, it is the lamp which hangs above the heavenly portal; thus, it cannot deceive. Upon what features fall its rays? Isaiah will help you. The light of understanding starkly reveals the valley of your disillusion, the mountain of your ambition, the rugged terrain of groundless anxiety, a moonscape of broken promises, injured feelings, missed opportunities, and self-doubt. This is the wilderness through which we all must pass. Even the saints were trapped now and then in a wasteland. They would not blame you for hiding from the penetrating rays, seeking the glittering distractions of shopping and parties, the non-reflective tinsel of December. At times the saints too felt unable to gaze unblinkingly upon the naked truth. But saint or sinner or a bit of both, we must turn back to the truth either by our own volition or compelled by the justice of God. By his grace, we shall find the other side of understanding, the consolation of the Holy Spirit.

The lamp of understanding is like a landlocked lighthouse. As its beam sweeps over the crags and nettles of your life, it also reveals the straight path heralded by Isaiah, that bound-for-glory road that wends its way through the mountains and valleys. It may not seem straight to you; it may indeed baffle you with changes in direction, 90° turns, dips, and reverses. But it is your path laid out by God and, in his eye, straight as an arrow flying to the golden door. Like a lighthouse, understanding illuminates your path intermittently, the beam interrupted by vain cares and false beginnings and specious dreams of fulfillment. The quiet times of Advent meditation slow the lamp's rotation permitting you to dwell upon the consolation of the path to God, the glory road.

Seek understanding today. Welcome this second gift of the Spirit and be forewarned of the pain which the lamp of truth can cause in your world of distractions. The cure is simple to prescribe but so hard to carry out. Bulldoze those shadowed structures of sin in your life. Level those outcroppings and ravines which impede truth and trap understanding. Make your path as straight as you can. When the beam from heaven's gate falls upon it, you shall know it is the Lord's path. Upon it he wishes to meet you.

Here begins the Gospel journey,
fitful lightning marks the way,
blazing eyes of John the Baptist
holding shades of doubt at bay.

Royal road but oddly narrow
mandates a most careful tread,
step by step on rugged sharp-edged
stones unsteady in their bed.

Wild, the prophet in his hurry
to reveal the journey's end
while the Master falls behind the
pace set by his restless friend.

God's own Lamb moves insecurely
toward his shadowed destiny
wondering if desert cousins
lose their sense of what should be.

If the son of Mary minds the
ruts and eyes the shifting sand,
is there blame for those who follow
fearful of the promised land?

Almighty God, Goal and Guide, guard our steps as we find our way around the pitfalls of life. Let us not stray back into the wasteland, but give us the lamp of understanding to light our way to you. Amen.

MONDAY OF THE SECOND WEEK

Jesus said, "Which is easier to say, 'Your sins are forgiven you,' or to say, 'Get up and walk'? In any case, to make it clear to you that the Son of Man has authority on earth to forgive sins" — he then addressed the paralyzed man: "I say to you, get up! Take your mat with you, and return to your house" (Lk 5:23-24).

One of the most striking paradoxes of Advent is the clash between the serenity of the songs of the season and the blare of what has become known as "pre-Christmas hype." Advertisers are in an orgy of activity — alluring, bombarding, compelling the customer. How sad it is that the come-on is so frequently accompanied by hymns that won't be validly sung until late on December 24th. What angels have heard on high is not a new stereo set. What shepherds come to adore is not a new blender. It is natural to seek respite from this crass display, to search out a place of peaceful communion with Christ who is the same yesterday, today, and forever. He will calm our jangled nerves and teach us the truths of the season in his soothing, predictable fashion.

Wait! That's not what today's Gospel says. When the friends of the paralyzed man placed him before Jesus, they expected a physical cure. Based on the reputation of this Galilean wonderworker, a timely recovery for their friend was a reasonable hope. Even the scribes and Pharisees would not have been surprised if Jesus had brought about a physical cure. There were magicians in the country who seemed to do the same things. Jesus, however, confounded Pharisees, scribes, friends, and paralytic alike. He did the unexpected, and pronounced the man forgiven.

When you ask of the Lord his gift of peace in this season, don't be too calculating, don't make him fit your scenario. If you pull the blinds in your prayer place, lock the door, assume your favorite meditation posture, and wait for his word, be prepared for the unexpected. The Prince of Peace may have a different witness for you to give this day. He may very well need a messenger to go forth into those noisy streets and that crass commercialism to bring his peace where it has never been felt before. The prayer gifts he has given you in the past are not yours to hoard. Expect the unexpected when it comes to Emmanuel. If God can become man, certainly we should not be surprised at any of his subsequent wonders. Can he not commission you — a Christian seeking greater peace in a season of material clatter — to spread the peace his grace has already brought you upon the raucous hype of December? He can and he may, but we know not when or if.

It is no sin to seek a quiet place of peace in this or any other season. It was no sin for the paralytic's friends to seek a physical cure for him. It was no sin for the scribes and Pharisees to expect such a cure. Nor was Jesus trying to outsmart the Pharisees or befuddle his friends or in any other way prove his superiority. He simply saw a greater need, a need which outweighed the wonder of walking again. Jesus saw that the man needed to be forgiven, and he would have left it at the shriving if the scribes and Pharisees had not been so obtuse. He cured the physical paralysis only to show that he had cured the spiritual paralysis.

In Advent we prepare to celebrate the most unexpected event the world had ever witnessed. In anticipation of that feast, make yourself available to the Lord so that he might work wonders in you and through you. Given the preponderance of needs outside your prayer place, the chances are good that, once or twice during this month, you will be led into the chaos of the season to bestow the kiss of peace upon some fevered brow. Expect the unexpected.

> If deserts bloom and steppes exult,
> the hobbled leap, the blinded see,
> if frightened hearts are girt with steel
> and slaves in Pharaoh's grip set free,
> if burning sands become sweet pools
> and wolf and lamb sit down to tea,
> if earthly-born is God's own son,
> then naught of his surprises me.

*Lord of the dance, delight us with the unexpected eruption of your
love in the most solemn chambers of our hearts. Let the fluttering of
your Spirit's wings tickle and confound those who would make of life
an endless cycle of dour duty and lowering glances.   Amen.*

TUESDAY OF THE SECOND WEEK

Jesus said, "What is your thought on this: A man owns a
hundred sheep and one of them wanders away; will he not leave
the ninety-nine out on the hills and go in search of the stray?"
(Mt 18:12).

The pensioners sat in the leather chairs scattered around
the lobby of the small residential hotel. Now and then, one
of the old men would match the creak of his bones to the
screech of the leather, rise painfully to his feet, and shuffle
to the frosty window. With the cuff of his best coat to clear a
spot through which the approach of any carriage could be
seen, he would give the peeling porte-cochere the briefest of
glances and then move slowly around the lobby before re-
suming his protesting chair.
      Even behind the heavy oak registration desk, the
proprietor heard the bells on the horses long before any of
his elderly guests. New business was nonexistent on Christmas Eve, so he amused himself with guessing games. Would
a family member come in to fetch the old man? Most often,
it was a servant, but sometimes one of the grandchildren,
never the son or daughter. Would they come in a carriage or
a sleigh? And who would be left? Nearly every Christmas, a
carriage departed without a passenger after the expectant
guest was gravely informed of unforeseen and unfortunate
circumstances.

This year there were no sleighs. Although the weather was quite cold for December, snow had been sparse. This year, one little girl, one little boy, and four servants brought icy gusts into the lobby. In the space of thirty minutes, six old men went out into the night. One stayed in his chair until seven o'clock. Then, with a sigh, he went to his room on the third floor after telling the proprietor that it was "probably sickness." At seven-thirty, that diagnosis was found wanting when a footman told the proprietor before he went upstairs that three carriageloads of young people had descended on the house and quite a party was in progress. The mister and missus were dining alone in their rooms. After the footman came down and left the lobby, the proprietor put the service bell out and went back to his quarters to tell his wife what she was accustomed to hearing. "Who is it this year?" "Mr. Randolph."

She was resigned to it now. She hadn't argued the point for years. "Have you asked him yet?" "No, I wanted to see how you felt first." She felt as she always did at having an intruder at their festive table. She felt just like her two sons looked as they sat glumly by the fireplace listening to this familiar dialogue, knowing the outcome. She felt that even Pastor Mitchell's wife didn't have to put up with this, locked with her fraud of a husband in the impregnable house on the hill. She didn't say any of this. She wanted to spare her husband from having to tell the family that he didn't like it any more than they, that he couldn't let old Mr. Randolph sit through Christmas Eve alone in his room, that this was part of doing business. She said abruptly, "Go up and ask him."

The boys grumbled but did their part: another leaf in the big table, the fifth setting of grandma's china, more wood in the box, the ottoman from the storeroom for the old gent's gouty feet. They hoped this year that they would be spared a whole evening of futile conversation with a deaf old fogey. If Dad would only send these strays away after the meal. But, no, they had to be part of the family. After all, this was Christmas. The boys tried to remember the last real family Christmas Eve. They went back ten years before they could picture the table around which just the four of them sat.

After a rather long wait, punctuated by covers rattling on the boiling pots, the resigned hostess said that everything was ready and where was Dad. "And where's Mr. Randolph?" she said ten minutes later when her husband returned alone. "He said he'd rather not and for us to go ahead without him."

It had to be the best Christmas meal in . . . well, in ten years. The family was drawn together by warm memories. The dark wine brought a blush to everyone's cheeks. Even Dad seemed to relax for the first time in weeks as the family focussed their loving attention on him. He felt like Father Christmas. Not until dessert was served was there renewed curiosity about Mr. Randolph. This time, the proprietor said that he had been invited home after all. He wondered if they had noticed the change in the story, and when he should notify Doc Barnes about the body.

celestial shepherd prods the earth
with crook of lightning overturns
each heap of sorrow mound of loss
that bury lonely souls beneath
serene horizons of the sleek

celestial shepherd calls them forth
black sheep emerge with starry eyes
from solitary catacombs
sure only of the sweet command
to find their place among his fold

Good Shepherd, I ask today for the certainty that comes only from humble submission to your loving guidance. Call me from prideful abandon to right conduct, from self-seeking to self-giving. Lead me to your pastures of peace. Amen.

WEDNESDAY OF THE SECOND WEEK

Jesus said: "Come to me, all you who are weary and find life burdensome, and I will refresh you. Take my yoke upon your shoulders and learn from me, for I am gentle and humble of heart. Your souls will find rest, for my yoke is easy and my burden light" (Mt 11:28-30).

Look at the Stations of the Cross in your church and see Jesus crushed to the earth beneath his burden. Read in your Bible about those who walked with him no more when he unburdened himself of the truth about his mission. Picture him weeping from the pain of a heart burdened with disappointment over Jerusalem. Again and again from Bethany to Nazareth to Calvary, Jesus is staggered by the death of a friend, the rejection of a home town, the vindictiveness of a nation. Is any part of this the light burden and easy yoke about which Jesus speaks in today's Gospel? The question is more than academic. As part of our quest for the peace of this season, we must decide what shall be our reply to his invitation to take his yoke upon our shoulders.

It seems counterproductive. Each of us can agree with Jesus' description of mankind as "you who are weary and find life burdensome." We certainly yearn for the refreshment he promises. But can we be refreshed by taking on yet another yoke and another burden? The answer is "yes." The password is "trust." We must trust Jesus and learn from him.

If he says he will refresh us, he will do it. If he says his yoke is easy and his burden light, it will be so for us. Scripture reveals that Jesus is not asking us to carry his cross. It was neither light nor easy. It was so heavy that it drove him to the ground. We are to take up our own crosses. Nor is Jesus asking us to bear the infinitely more crushing burden of mankind's sins. They crushed him to death. We are to bear our own guilt. The yoke and the burden he speaks of in today's Gospel is his total submission to his Father's will.

Total submission to God's will does not make the pain of your arthritis any less. It does not ease those pangs of envy that arise when someone else gets the new car or the better job. It does not fill the hole in your heart left by your departed spouse. These are sharp points of the everyday burdens and yokes that come with being human. Jesus chose to be human and paid the price. Each of you reading these words is human and must suffer the human condition no matter how total your submission to God's will.

In the midst of life's suffering, you can choose merely to survive or you can choose to grow; you have the opportunity simply to endure the trial or to become more spiritually mature. Submission to God's will doesn't mean rolling over and playing dead, but deliberately choosing the path of Jesus and actively deciding to make your suffering redemptive. As he suffered and died in complete submission to his Father's will, and thereby merited the crown of resurrection, so you can merit eternal life and help others to know resurrection by submitting to God's will, no matter how great the test, and witnessing to your faith in his power and compassion. Jesus gave us resurrection but we can't really see or touch resurrection. What is tangible to us about his gift is his nobility and trust during his suffering, the result of his submission to his Father. Your example of the same submission under duress — whether it be a life-threatening situation or some routine plan gone awry — manifests a nobility of character that can sway everyone who comes close to you. Think of the redemptive deaths of saintly people ravaged by the most hideous illness or injury. Like Jesus, they move others to faith because of their submission to God's will. They accept the invitation to "take my yoke upon your shoulder and learn from me," and in so doing become as "gentle and humble of heart" as is the Redeemer. They become, in fact, redeemers, conforming their lives to his and their wills to that of his Father as they nobly accept the responsibility for others. Their example of trust in trial melts the stony heart of the scoffer. They gladly submit to God's plan and find the burden light and the yoke easy. Learn from them. Learn from their Teacher.

> Until it is heated
> the wax will not yield
> to the signet of gold.
>
> Until it is kneaded
> the dough will not rest
> in the shape of the mold.
>
> Until it is heeded
> God's word cannot fill
> empty hearts stony cold.

Redeemer King, you made of human suffering a high calling and taught us to bear our burdens for the sake of those who need to see your Father's power in our weakness. May we learn anew your lessons of obedience and trust, and join our sorrows to yours for the salvation of the world.   Amen.

THURSDAY OF THE SECOND WEEK

Jesus said to the crowds: "I solemnly assure you, history has
not known a man born of woman greater than John the Baptizer.
Yet the least born into the kingdom of God is greater than he.
From John the Baptizer's time until now the kingdom of God
has suffered violence, and the violent take it by force"
(Mt 11:11-12).

Yesterday's meditation on submission to God's will leads
naturally to the discovery of that rare gem, peace. The
submission that brings true peace must not be confused with
quietism, a kind of sitting on one's moral hands lest they
flutter upward in disobedience to the divine mandate. Submission here means active conformance to the will of God.
This kind of submission is as dynamic as was that prowling
lion of the desert, John the Baptizer. John had been one of
those about whom Jesus spoke in today's Gospel, a man who
would take the kingdom of God by violence. John was a
shouting preacher of repentance. Today, he would probably be lumped with those who cry, "Back to the Bible!" He
cut himself off from the ease of the cities and stood alone at
the Jordan River daring sinners to come forward and accept
the bath of repentance as it flowed through his hands. The
last of the Old Testament prophets, he perceived his calling
as a duty to pull out by the roots the corrupt growths of
political collaboration and religious assimilation which
choked the full flowering of pristine Judaism.

Then one day he saw the world turn upside down as his
cousin came to the Jordan to seek his baptism. The wings of
a dove, a voice from above meant a new age had begun. God
remained the same, but the shape of John's vocation had
changed; he would have to conform to this new command.
Now, violence would be done to him; his plans would be

roughly recast; he would be no longer the heralded but the herald. John made the transition. His desert ministry was gradually abandoned as he pointed to his cousin as the Lamb of God. Evil, in the guise of King Herod, hurried the process. At the end, John of the desert, who so forcefully preached and exemplified renunciation, became the victim of a violent man and a woman who personified avarice.

Meditate today on what it cost John the Baptizer to say "Yes" to his new calling, to say publicly that he was not worthy to loosen his cousin's sandal strap. From the dynamic desert preacher, he changed not to supine jellyfish but to loyal pathfinder. He actively reshaped his will to God's new revelation. This is the kind of deliberate and vital submission that we must cultivate in our own lives if we are to know the peace of this season. This single-hearted submission to God's will brings with it the calmness of conscience and the serenity of outlook which comprise the easy yoke and light burden to which Jesus invites us.

Scripture tells us that Herod was fascinated by his prisoner. "When he heard him speak he was very much disturbed; yet he felt the attraction of his words" (Mk 6:20). What would both disturb and attract a man whose greed was so great that only violence could procure what he wanted? Another man at peace! The repose of John in prison, that aura of serenity in the face of dire peril, the calm strength which withstood all threats — this was the mystery of the Baptizer, this was the grail which Herod sought but could not comprehend. This is the grail we all seek, the fruit of active conformance with God's will. This kind of peace doesn't come from holding your principles in suspended animation, but from sometimes painfully matching the shape of your decision to the shape of God's law. It doesn't come easily; it requires a daily struggle to submit your choices to the Just Judge. Peace is knowing that you are

trying to do God's will. Like John the Baptizer, you will find
your peace in the striving.

It wafted from
a prison cell
this threat of peace
that casts a spell
upon a king
unmanned by fear
of learning what
this desert seer
might think of his
pernicious ways
as farther from
the Law he strays.

Here peace is curse
on Herod's plan
disturbs his sleep
prevents the man
from shaping gods
to do his will
for never shall
his heart be still
if to submit
as John well shows
is Yahweh's path
to sweet repose.

*Lord, rescue your people from hostility and violence. Send us out to
sow the still, small seed of peace in this contentious world. Nurture
its growth with the bright sun of your justice and the gentle rain of
your mercy. Bless us finally with the privilege of working in the
harvest.   Amen.*

FRIDAY OF THE SECOND WEEK

Thus says the Lord, your redeemer,
the Holy One of Israel:
I, the Lord, your God,
teach you what is for your good,
and lead you on the way you should go (Is 48:17).

One sign of age is the loss of spontaneity. Deliberate, measured steps mark the passage of each year. "Watch your step." "Conserve your strength." Every action, every decision is thoroughly thought through and all possibilities investigated. The result is that many older people become prisoners of caution. They contract fatal dullness and die of self-inflicted boredom.

The same lack of spontaneity can occur in one's prayer life regardless of age. I remember in my teen years going to Mass or the Stations of the Cross and nearly dying of boredom. Too little life in my prayer life made it a chore. There are periods in everyone's pilgrimage when he or she needs a change of pace in prayer. Today, we seek that spiritual spontaneity which is a concommitant of counsel, the third of the pre-Christmas gifts of the Holy Spirit.

Counsel, in the context of prayer, is that impulse of the Holy Spirit which gives us confidence that we are doing the right thing when we pray. It is a sense of certainty that is ours without a great deal of deliberation or examination. It is ultimately a deep, loving trust in God, and an unshakable belief that he desires to hear us and speak to us. This confidence gives us the freedom to pray without constantly looking over our shoulders to see if we've taken the correct path to prayer. The Holy Spirit's gift of counsel allows us to be spontaneous in prayer.

When, in our passage from Isaiah, the Lord says through his prophet that he will teach us what is for our good and lead us on the way we should go, he is promising the gift of counsel. Those who accept that gift will find it easy to follow the urgings of the Holy Spirit. They will be freed of the usual constraints on their prayer life. They will trust their divine guide to bring them closer to himself. Since they will worry less about the theories and methods of prayer, they will find a new kind of peace in prayer.

Test that peace today. Let a bit of spontaneity into your meditation. If you are accustomed to kneel, sit instead. Substitute spontaneous prayers for the formulas you've been using for so long. Have you ever sung your prayer? Ever stood with arms upraised? Ever emptied your mind of every thought and concentrated on a chirping bird? The point is to do something different today. Rely on the gift of counsel to lead you in the right way. You need not promise to pray this way tomorrow. Let counsel lead you tomorrow. Today, pray as if there were no tomorrow. Express yourself to God as an incarnation of his best idea of you. You are here with all your qualities and foibles because he put you here. In your heart, perhaps buried way down deep, is a bit of freedom. It is a part of you that God loves very much. Show it to him. Don't be afraid. He gave you spontaneity; now he sends you the gift of counsel so that you can trust yourself to him and with him and in him. Don't be anxious about words or posture or distractions or the clock. Don't be anxious about anything. Please God by praying free.

Free to be
    to be me
        shaking in the shadowed church.
Unconstrained
    angels rained
        bolts of joy upon the roof.
Blocked by tin
    and the din
        of the tolling, droning words,
dancing grace
    upped the pace,
        split the shingle, cracked the beam
and quite soon
    poured the moon
        over my constricted soul
drenching one
    grateful son
        with a love unrealized.
Now I yearn
    to return
        to that night of doubt and awe,
free to be
    to be me
        waiting in the shadowed church.

Lord and Liberator, free me to rejoice with you over the goodness of our heavenly Father. Make me a herald of the Good News, a messenger of love and life, a sign among your people of the freedom of the kingdom come.   Amen.

SATURDAY OF THE SECOND WEEK

Jesus said: "I assure you, though, that Elijah has already come, but they did not recognize him and they did as they pleased with him. The Son of Man will suffer at their hands in the same way." The disciples then realized that he had been speaking to them about John the Baptizer (Mt 17:12-13).

The phrase, "they did as they pleased with him," always makes me think of the dog that catches the toad. For a while, he plays with his prey, but the match is so uneven that boredom sets in, the teeth come out, and the toad is dismembered. They did as they pleased with John the Baptizer, but tired of the sport. His severed head became the centerpiece of a new diversion, a more shocking entertainment. All because they didn't recognize him. The dog thinks the toad is a like-minded playmate. When he learns his hope for good sport will be denied, he gets rid of his disappointment. Herod and his henchmen thought John the Baptizer was an exotic, yet harmless, rustic philosopher. When his remarks struck the royal family, he was silenced by imprisonment. Silence made John very boring. The sport was over. They had done as they pleased with him; he pleased them no more.

When our world asks why good Christians become concerned at the prospect of a Christmas celebration spread over the four preceding weeks, the answer is precisely this: Advent is a season of preparation; Christmas is that event for which we prepare. To intermingle the preparation with the celebration is to recognize the full significance of neither.

Like the dog with the toad, we spend a month playing with Christmas, doing as we please with it. We wear out Christmas long before the calendar announces its arrival. In the chaos of shopping and parties and decorating, we have little time for prayerful meditation on the Incarnation. How many people finally drag themselves to December 25th, pull the back of their hand across their brow and say, "Thank God, that's over!"? Nearly every year, what little spiritual solace we can wring out of these four weeks comes early, perhaps even before this day, the midpoint of Advent. We have done what we pleased with this season; we have toyed with it in prayer and caught a fleeting glimpse of an ancient world preparing for a redeemer. There have been consolations, but now when the world commands our return to the business of Christmas, we must end the sport, dismember our ideals, and give ourselves totally to the frenzy of these last two weeks.

No, not this year. Let today be not merely a midpoint but a turning point. Choose not to become Jacob Marley's ghost, laden with coins and purses and chains of gold. Instead, admit that up to now you did as you pleased with this misunderstood season. This is the day to repent of your cavalier treatment of Advent and to resolve to make these last two weeks a time of spiritual growth. Celebrate *Advent!*

How does one begin to celebrate Advent? Recognition is important. The dog toyed with the toad because he thought it was a playmate. Herod tolerated John because he mistook him for a country seer. We do as we please with this season because we believe it is a four-week Christmas Eve. See Advent for what it is: a time of quiet waiting and preparation for the birth of the Prince of Peace, a time to be pregnant with the life of Christ waiting to be born into your world, a womb-time to contemplate, to wonder at the miracle that saw light two thousand years ago and can come to life in you again. During these two weeks, you have it in your power to be mother to peace in that sector of the universe which you call your world. Recognize Advent for what it is: a gentle, fragile, protected time when peace forms fingers and toes, and ponders in the dark what kind of world is waiting.

God understands how the tinsel and carols can fool you. He forgives you for doing with this season what you pleased. Now that you have recognized the discrete beauty of Advent, it is not too late for an intensive preparation for the birth of peace in your heart. Reorganize your priority list. Put last minute shopping and raucous gatherings at the bottom of the list. At the top, describe your own quiet place where dreams of peace can gestate. Then find that place.

> The iceman dreamed in the snowstorm
>> of crystal beaches
>> summer and sport
>> pail and sand
>> and warm
>> sun.
>
> The parson dreamed in the pulpit
>> of people heeding
>> incense and bells
>> eyes and ears
>> and new
>> faith.
>
> The virgin dreamed in the desert
>> of verdant pastures
>> lions and lambs
>> dates and figs
>> and cool
>> rain.

The God-man dreamed in the darkness
    of happy children
    value and need
    hope and love
    and sweet
    peace.

Father of new beginnings, renew our faith in Advent. We resolve to make of this season a time of preparation for the coming of the Prince of Peace. Help us to find that quiet place where hope can grow undisturbed.   Amen.

THIRD SUNDAY OF ADVENT

Rejoice always, never cease praying, render constant
thanks; such is God's will for you in Christ Jesus
(1 Th 5:16-18).

Joy. Prayer. Thanksgiving. St. Paul's exhortation to the Christians at Thessalonika is a succinct sketch of what Advent should be. Obviously, this should be a season of prayer. To a place apart trudge the weary pilgrims, there to be refreshed by sweet communion with the Lord. A beautiful idea, the realization of which requires for the modern man and woman a series of small miracles: the miracle of time in a busy schedule, the miracle of silence in a noisy world, the miracle of patience in a Quik-Stop society. Yet, none of this is impossible with God. He is the maker of miracles. If Advent has been for you up to now a season of frustration, do not despair. Your inability to find that quiet place, those twenty serene minutes, that calm anticipation of a consoling word is not a sign that you are meant to languish beyond

God's reach. Your frustration is one way God reaches a person and shakes him or her up. God does not send the noise, the hassle, or the impatience; rather, he uses these slings and arrows of outrageous fortune to call your attention to what you have overlooked. You sought the silence, squeezed your schedule for the time, stifled your impatience, but forgot the other half of Paul's advice to the Thessalonians. "Rejoice always, never cease praying, render constant thanks; such is God's will for you *in Christ Jesus*."

In Christ Jesus. . . . Everything we do should be done in Christ Jesus, that is, according to the way of Christ. Was Jesus ever frustrated in his prayer? I can't think of an occasion in the New Testament when he wasn't. Again and again he goes apart to pray, sometimes taking his closest followers with him, sometimes not. Shortly, either the crowds find him and besiege him with pleas or, if he manages to elude the crowds, the disciples make it agonizingly clear that they really don't know what he is all about and certainly aren't on his wavelength when it comes to prayer. A sad example would be the series of prayers which began at the Last Supper and ended in Gethsemane. Nearly all the Scriptural utterances of Jesus in the Upper Room were in the context of prayer, prayer offered in counterpoint to the blatant obtuseness of his closest friends and the ongoing betrayal of one of them. Then to the Garden. Here he endured physical weakness, spiritual loneliness, and a final interruption by a crowd seeking his arrest. Praying in Christ Jesus, then, means praying according to his way, and his way included the same imperfect environment that frustrates you. It's called the world. Praying in Christ Jesus means keeping on despite the noise, rush, and impatience. God's will for you is never to cease praying, that is, never to give up praying as Jesus prayed. Take heart from the knowledge that he has been there.

The same holds true for the constant thanks and unceasing joy which Paul urges upon the Thessalonians. Is Advent a season of preparation or joy? Both. The deep, quiet joy which should be ours during this season is born of our confidence that what we hope for has already come to pass. The world has received its Savior. Now we make our hearts ready to receive him anew. Our joy is according to God's will in Christ Jesus. We are happy the way Jesus was happy when he welcomed a follower who accepted him as the fulfillment of the law and the prophets. Even in the midst of a world which seems to go out of its way to create sadness, in quiet joy we busy ourselves with the task of making our hearts fit dwelling places for the Prince of Peace. Our nearly hidden smile reveals that we are happy in Christ Jesus.

Thanksgiving is our constant calling. No matter what the season, we can never finish counting our blessings according to the way of Jesus. His gratitude was always too big for words; in healing, blessing, forgiving, sacrificing, he gave thanks to his Father by making whole again his Father's sons and daughters. You and I, as Christians who have seen God's promises kept, can be thankful in advance during Advent. We know this earth is being filled with the Savior. He grows larger each time he is born into another heart. He has been born in ours and we prepare to welcome him again. An important part of our preparation involves showing our gratitude to God by helping his children to prepare to receive a divine gift. This was Jesus' way of giving thanks. We do the same according to God's will in Christ Jesus. God's gifts are seen in our giving.

Joy. Prayer. Thanksgiving. All *in Christ Jesus.* Advent is a time to conform our will to God's will for us. In Jesus, we see that perfect conformity in the face of all the challenges which the world could mount. With Jesus and in his world, we rejoice in the coming of the Prince of Peace, give thanks that our Father made his coming possible, and pray that the possibility will be realized in our hearts. Joy, prayer, thanksgiving: Advent.

> Minor miracles
> line the landscape of the soul
> tracing out to all who heed
> God's reign burgeoning
>
> Petty prodigies
> marked by few along the way
> undervalued up against
> man's technology
>
> Tiny testaments
> to refute the master plan
> tendrils set the data bank's
> dials a'quivering
>
> Fragile filaments
> strands of tears and tenderness
> stretching past the cold machines
> bind the world in love

God among us, help us to see and appreciate the everyday wonders you work in our midst. Extend your kingdom through your very ordinary servants. May we be humble heralds of the miracle called peace.   Amen.

*   *   *

Note on the Advent Calendar

Because Advent always begins on a Sunday but may end on any day of the week, the length of the season varies. It may be as short as twenty-two days or as long as twenty-eight days. From tomorrow forward, the reader should be alert to the calendar. On whatever day of the week December 17th or 18th occurs after the Third Sunday of Advent, the meditations for calendar *dates* should be used until Christmas, except for the Fourth Sunday. They begin on page 70.

MONDAY OF THE THIRD WEEK

Your ways, O Lord, make known to me;
     teach me your paths,
Guide me in your truth and teach me,
     for you are God my savior (Ps 25:4-5).

Lisa's problem was not unusual among second-year college students who called themselves Christians. She was losing her faith. At least that's what she told the campus minister on the first day of Christmas break. It was important enough for her to delay her homecoming by twenty-four hours in order to tell him the whole story. So she was surprised that their meeting was so brief. In less than half an hour, the chaplain had drawn out of her what she believed in, what she didn't, and the degree of her doubt. She believed in God, but wondered how good he could be in allowing so much tragedy in the world. She believed in prayer, but had felt for some time that it was without purpose or profit. She believed in going to church, but questioned rules about frequency of attendance. She believed in a moral standard, but hers was quite different now from what she had been taught. The minister let her know that he understood what she was going through, that her problem was important to him, and that he would enjoy taking the rest of the day to speak with her. But an intermediate step was necessary. He asked her to spend an hour in the students' chapel and answer a question which he proceeded to write on a sheet of paper. He folded the paper, gave Lisa a pen, and told her to return at 11:00 a.m.

As she sat on the hard pew, she wondered if the chaplain was giving her the brush-off. After all, he probably wanted to get home too. There were only a few words on the paper: "You told me what you believe and what you don't believe.

Now list on this paper what you think you SHOULD believe." After an hour of distraction, frustration, and a smidgen of soul-searching, she gave up. There were only four entries on her list: God, prayer, church, morals — the points of conflict she had discussed with the campus minister.

At 11:00 a.m., Lisa let him know that she hadn't gotten any farther than a resume of her doubts. "Thought it might be so," he said. "That *should* made all the difference. You are a *should* person. You know what you should believe in, what you ought to be doing, and, thank God, you are doing it. Go home and enjoy your vacation. Keep your oughts and your doubts in perspective and don't be troubled if they sound the same." He told her the story of the man who said to Jesus, "Lord, I believe; help my unbelief," and how that was every Christian's prayer. *Ought* and *doubt* are part of the struggle for spiritual fulfillment. Growth demands the thrust and parry of belief and its absence. He kept her list and told her to pray, "Lord, I believe; help my unbelief," each day of the Christmas break and not to worry too much over her doubts. It was the meaning of the prayer and her appreciation of it that was important.

With this prayer, Lisa would be invoking the Holy Spirit and calling down upon herself the fourth of his gifts, knowledge. Spiritual knowledge is that charism which enables us to identify what should be known by faith. This kind of knowledge illuminates the "ought" in the campus minister's guidance. As she prayed, Lisa would be enlightened by this gift of the Holy Spirit so that her confusion would lessen and her inner vision would clear. The chaplain wanted her to come to know what was important to the spiritual life of a twenty year old student at a state university and what beliefs were secondary now even though they might become important later.

Today in your Advent meditation, pray for the Holy Spirit's gift of knowledge. Pray that you may not be encumbered by massive doubts over little things. "Lord, I believe; help my unbelief" means that God, prayer, church, and morality are of utmost importance to you even though from time to time doubts creep into the spectrum of your faith. If you would know the peace of this season, you must not be caught in a whirlpool of questions. The Spirit's gift of knowledge helps you to see what objects of faith are important to you today, in this time and place. Rest in this knowledge. Be certain of one thing: Christ sends his Spirit not to accuse us of lack of faith but to help our unbelief.

As for Lisa, it would be nice to report that her faith grew stronger. That outcome is not certain because Lisa is still growing. It is too soon to tell where God is calling her. But this much is certain: If Lisa and you are still praying, "Lord, I believe; help my unbelief," you are both pilgrims on a journey to belief, faithful as you can be.

Your truth, O Lord, make known to us
as we recoil from whirling doubt
which mixes peace with giving up
while certainties are tossed about
cut free from their most holy source.
Tornadic is the skeptic's breath
exhaling disbelief upon
a gasping world that marks not death.

Upon the dust fall apse and spire.
Virginity is ridiculed.
Canned laughter muffles litanies.
Your love, your laws are overruled.
O, calm the storms that twist our faith.
Extend, my God, your mighty hand
to touch and orient our quest
to find the truth and take a stand.

Father of the faithful, preserve us in our belief, guide us in the quest
for truth, strengthen us in giving witness to the faith we hold dear.
We, who are searchers, give thanks for the lamp of knowledge which
your Holy Spirit bears before us.   Amen.

TUESDAY OF THE THIRD WEEK

Jesus said to them, "Let me make it clear that tax collectors
and prostitutes are entering the kingdom of God before you.
When John came preaching a way of holiness, you put no faith
in him; but the tax collectors and the prostitutes did believe in
him. Yet even when you saw that, you did not repent and
believe in him" (Mt 21:31-32).

We all know people with short tempers. When the un-
wary wave the red flag, the sand flies in the bull ring. We
know when to keep that flag furled, but sometimes stand
aside and let a newcomer learn a lesson. Jesus was not a
newcomer on the subject of the chief priests and elders of
the people. He knew all the ways to trigger their anger and
did just that from time to time to make a point and teach a
lesson. The most tender of subjects was obedience to the
Law. Most good Jews and their leaders believed that those
branded as public sinners — tax collectors and prostitutes,
for example — were despicable in the eyes of Yahweh and
had little, if any, chance of entering his kingdom. Jews
obedient to the Law, and especially their leaders, were
guaranteed entry. So in today's Gospel, when Jesus stands
the collective wisdom on its head, the chief priests and elders
are livid with rage and try to have Jesus arrested.
     We may chuckle at the perplexity of the Jewish leaders.
Since they are not able to refute Jesus, they could only

attempt violence. They could not refute him because they knew that they themselves were sinners. Though they gave the Law external reverence, their hearts were filled with pride of place, their coffers with Temple offerings, their days with the preservation of the status quo. That they were caught on the horns of a dilemma called hypocrisy warms our hearts and renews our faith in God's justice.

Until we think of our own situation. . . . You probably know few public sinners, but you are acquainted with several obvious, albeit private, ones: the alcoholic uncle, the cursing brother-in-law, the philandering boss, the gouging land-lord. Would they be able to enter God's kingdom before you who keep his laws? Could these, who brazenly flout God's will, know salvation while you, who attend church regularly, languish in the outer darkness? The answer is "Yes, if . . .," if they repent and you don't.

The public sinners with whom Jesus consorted were those who reformed their lives and turned to him. Your uncle, brother-in-law, boss, and landlord have received the same invitation and can seek the same transformation in their lives. The chief priests and elders, on the other hand, were convinced of their own salvation because of their out-ward adherence to the Law and thus saw no need of repent-ance. Can you see yourself in their number? You may be a church worker, a regular participant in the liturgy, even a weekly communicant, and still be a *surface* Christian, one who shows up well in the parish *Who's Who*, yet is filled with pride, envy, ambition — all the seeds which spring forth into the ugliest of blooms, hypocrisy.

Advent is not a season for smugness. It is for a "people humble and lowly" of whom Zephaniah speaks in today's first reading, those who "take refuge in the name of the Lord" (Zp 3:12). To be humble and lowly is to admit your failings and to repent of them. To be humble and lowly is to be like the Virgin Mary who obediently bowed to God's will and thus became the preeminent bearer of the Good News. The chief priests, the elders, the scribes, the Pharisees — so many of the Jewish leaders could not recognize who Jesus was because they would not admit who they really were. Their tragic mistake was to think they were better than those who knew they were worse and admitted it. Because the Jewish leaders could not admit their hypocrisy, they could not repent of it. Because they could not repent, they could not confess their sin. Because they could not confess, they could not be forgiven. They had managed with all their guile to commit the unforgivable sin. In contrast, the public sinners who followed Jesus did so because he helped them admit, repent, and confess. Then he forgave them. He will do the same for you. Turn to him today and take three very necessary steps in preparing your heart for the Prince of Peace. Admit. Repent. Confess. Jesus will take the fourth step. He will forgive you.

> Gangway! Here come the newly shorn,
> the rabble who amidst the din
> of freedom run amuck have heard
> the promise of forgiven sin.
>
> Stand clear, you whited sepulchers
> whose gleam external mocks the sun,
> you paragons of probity
> exemplars of the way it's done.
>
> Take care, for since you holier
> than thou disdained the inward glance,
> you'll find yourself beyond the pale,
> beseeching Him for one more chance.

Cry out beside the rude parade,
the great unwashed by Christ made clean.
Condemned are you like carrion crow
eternally to pick and preen.

Father of mercy, I have failed to match my deeds to my words, my actions to my faith, my love to my need. Judge me not as I judge others. As I stand trembling beneath your terrible justice, forgive my hypocrisy. Wash me clean in the blood of the Lamb. Amen.

WEDNESDAY OF THE THIRD WEEK

The disciples of John brought their teacher word of all these happenings. Summoning two of them, John sent them to ask the Lord, "Are you 'He who is to come' or are we to expect someone else?" (Lk 7:18-19).

John the Baptizer was becoming increasingly concerned. His cousin from Nazareth turned out to be less than he expected. John saw the kingdom of God as imminent and Jesus as the one who would call down God's punishment upon all who were not ready to accept the kingdom. Acceptance of the kingdom called for a renunciation of sin and a baptism of repentance. John preached renunciation and offered baptism in preparation for Jesus who would close the book on the present dispensation and separate the sheep from the goats. That's how John saw it; yet, now for months Jesus himself had been preaching repentance, as if John had somehow been less than persuasive, as if Jesus were just another dispenser of easy grace. Where was the fire in his eyes? Where was the judgment in his words? Might John even have ruefully concluded that the title, "Lamb of God," had been rather too apt? So he sent some of his followers to question Jesus, to find out if John had been mistaken in his hopes for an early dissolution of this corrupted world, to determine if the search should begin for another Messiah.

Jesus replied with a recitation of the works he was doing, then warned John about giving in to impatience. When Jesus called blessed the man who found no stumbling block in him, he was telling John to look at the big picture. "John," he was saying, "I know your zeal for the kingdom. I know your righteousness and your abhorrence of sin. But, John, Rome wasn't built in a day." You won't find this quotation in Scripture, but it is a fair elaboration of Jesus' disapproval of impatience, even John the Baptizer's *holy* impatience.

Advent could be called the *impatient* season, especially among the young who can hardly wait for presents or school vacations. Those of us who are older become impatient with long lines at checkout counters and interminable traffic jams. Our reaction to these delays can sometimes be discourteous, to say the least. But what about so-called holy impatience in this or any other season? We grow irritable when our prayers — prayers for quite noble ends — go unanswered. "Why doesn't God scare my son back into church?" We can't understand a lingering illness. "Why doesn't Jesus touch me with his healing hand?" Most worrisome are the ongoing moral outrages over which we have no control. "Only God can stop the scourge of terrorism, the cancer of pornography, the meaninglessness of suicide. Why doesn't he?"

Can you not hear the echo of your complaints in the question carried by John's followers? "Are we to expect someone else?" In other words, Jesus did not keep to John's timetable; he didn't bring down the wrath of God upon the heads of sinners. He was becoming a stumbling block to the impatient. Since you and I don't want to see God as a stumbling block in our grand design, we must know the reason for divine delay. The reason is in today's Gospel. "Go and report to John what you have seen and heard. The blind recover their sight, cripples walk, lepers are cured, the deaf hear, the dead are raised to life, and the poor have the good news preached to them" (Lk 7:22). If God seems to dally, it is only because he seeks to save. In his compassion for all, he wants to give the blind, the crippled, the leper, the deaf more time to turn to him for healing. He wants to give the sinner more time to repent. He wants to bring the dead to life even if they stink. Few, if any of us, suffer none of the above ills, failings, or misfortunes. Instead of focussing our wrath on all those others who are "getting away with murder" because of God's patience, we should thank him for tolerating our "little murders" and giving us the time to repent of them.

The delay, which nearly caused John the Baptizer to see in Jesus a stumbling block, should be our inspiration. If God, our sustainer, has every right to withdraw his hand because of our sins, and doesn't because of his patient mercy, then we should withhold our judgment of those who seem to be ripe for the reaper. Today, consider in a new light those who seem to offend God and certainly offend you; see them as experimental plants left to grow in their test beds while God sends his rain upon the good and the bad. These unruly growths may now possess all the characteristics of common weeds, but later. . . .? God who created the whole world from nothing and raised Jesus from the dead can certainly turn dandelions into wheat.

the clock ticks
without thought
of sorrow
or mercy

so just is
the timepiece
that nothing
can stop it

God's heart beats
in measures
now waxing
now waning

so patient
his justice
upon our
presumption

*Loving Lord, we give you thanks for your great mercy in spite of our
intolerance of the faults of others. Help us to see that which is godly in
each of our erring brothers and sisters. Let us be as patient with them
as you are with us.   Amen.*

THURSDAY OF THE THIRD WEEK

Raise a glad cry, you barren one who did not bear,
      break forth in jubilant song, you who were not in labor,
For more numerous are the children of the deserted wife
      than the children of her who has a husband,
         says the Lord (Is 54:1).

Few things frightened a Jewish husband more than the specter of dying without male issue. A man and his family lived on in spirit in their first-born son. This was as close as most Jews came to the concept of immortality. It is hard for us today to imagine the consuming interest regarding a woman's lineage or fecundity when it came to arranging a marriage. Nor can we fathom the depth of tragedy in the curse of barrenness. So it is with no small sense of surprise that we read the opening lines of today's first reading from the book of Isaiah.

In writing these words, the prophet's immediate aim was to prepare the Babylonian exiles for their return to Jerusalem. Virtually empty for seventy-five years, the city was now to be filled with the grandchildren of those who were banished by Nebuchadnezzar. In the sense of the season of Advent, however, this praise of barrenness can be seen as an exhortation to self-emptying, to a cleansing of the heart to prepare a dwelling place for the Lord.

Purification before a great feast has a long and honorable tradition. To celebrate the feast in the proper spirit, those things which would detract from holiness must be removed. Worthless goals, evil intentions, distracting involvements are expelled from the heart that longs for the presence of the Lord. Cleansing of the heart by purification and penance produces the holy barrenness praised by the prophet.

The goal, though, is not mere purification but preparation for a hoped-for result: fecundity, re-creation, new life. As the tree is pruned to produce new growth and the field held fallow to bring forth a richer crop, so the heart is made empty to receive the living God. Who better exemplifies the merit of self-emptying than the Blessed Virgin Mary who, in company with a long line of childless women of the Old Testament, was made ready for the overshadowing of

Yahweh's spirit? As our Advent model, Mary breaks forth with the glad cry which the prophet urged upon Jerusalem. Hers is the jubilant song of all those who keep themselves apart, waiting in humble submission for the chance to say "Yes" to the Lord.

Now is the time to gauge your emptiness, to take stock of your readiness to receive the Prince of Peace. Recall those circumstances and situations in your life which seemed at first to be God's curse upon you, but later proved to be the slap of a reckless world in which God hid the touch of his love. How many heartbreaks have you had that led to new beginnings? How many setbacks which forced you to find your deeper, better self? How many tragic losses which eventually revealed a new and richer appreciation of life? Hidden in each of these crises and failures was God's invitation to empty yourself and cling only to him. In every circumstance which you felt powerless to change was an opportunity which God used to purify you of the sin of pride. Each situation which you were at a loss to influence let God lead you in his way, for a change. Then, trial and suffering imposed by a heartless world forced a purification of your self. Now, in this peaceful hour, you have the privilege of working with God in emptying your self of self. You will agree that this way is much to be preferred.

Begin today to seek this holy barrenness, this fallow field in which the Holy Spirit will plant the seed of divine life. Take every step possible, from prayer, sacrifice, fasting, and almsgiving to repentance and confession of your sins. Your soul must be washed clean of any corrupting growth, your heart must be cleansed of pride and self-conceit, your very life must be laid bare to be beheld only by your Father-Creator. Raise a glad cry that tragedy is not necessary to make you submissive. Break forth in jubilant song that in this quiet place, in this Peaceful Season, in this God-graced

moment, you can prepare a fit dwelling place for his Son.
You, who are barren and without child, can bring into your
world Peace-made-flesh.

Above the earth
the Spirit crooned,
to dancing set
the lark, the oak,
gazelles and men.

Once Sarah laughed
to hear such sport,
a song of life
that echoed in
her empty womb.

Elizabeth,
so old and gray,
did step and twirl
a *horah* set
to life in bloom.

God's music filled
that Mary born
immaculate,
quite barren of
all but desire.

And still His song
is heard today
in hearts that yearn
to bring to earth
the Prince of Peace.

God, Creator and Sustainer, help us to see in the tragedies which befall us the hidden flame of your love. May the purifying fire of suffering cleanse us of all which is unworthy of our high calling — the vocation of Christ-bearer, herald of peace, messenger of mercy. Amen.

FRIDAY OF THE THIRD WEEK

Them I will bring to my holy mountain
and make joyful in my house of prayer;
Their holocausts and sacrifices
will be acceptable on my altar,
For my house shall be called
a house of prayer for all peoples (Is 56:7).

With Christmas just a few days away, the pressures on many people become unbearable. Last minute shopping, wrapping, labeling, mailing, menu planning, party arrangements, the glut of saccharine carols oozing out of the radio, Christmas shows on television with outlandish celebrities in exotic locales. . . . It's enough to make a Scrooge of any Christian. You want to stand in the center of the busiest intersection in town and scream, "That's not what it's all about!" But nobody would pay you any mind. They would be mesmerized by the mechanical Santa in the department store window as he kneels at the Christ-child's crib.

There is a place in which to put this madness into perspective: your church. If you haven't been able to make these meditations in church, it is quite understandable. Your job schedule, school hours, distance may not permit you to go to church when it is open. Today, however, make the effort. Do some rearranging of your priorities. Create the time to rest in the Real Presence of the Living Lord there for you behind the golden doors of the tabernacle.

Can there be any greater peace than that which is ours in the immediate presence of the Blessed Sacrament? Of course, Christ is with his saints no matter where they may roam. He is God's love resting on our hearts when a friend betrays us. He is God's protection as we travel down the highway. He is God's healing hand touching us as we lie on our bed of pain. Godly people are people who know that God reveals himself every moment of the day. But this place called a church, this holy house, this house of prayer is the tangible center of the community's belief. The people of God have gathered stone and wood and mortar and brick to localize God's presence, to focus it, to celebrate it, to build a place where you and I can gather to ratify our belief in Emmanuel, God-with-us.

A church is the only place where the presence of one person can be called a holy gathering. When you sit alone near the tabernacle, you are sitting with Jesus at the focal point of peace in your community. You have presented your whole self — body, mind, heart, and soul — to the Father *in union* with the whole self — body, blood, soul, and divinity — of Jesus. You have gathered with Jesus in honor of your common Father. There is no other place and no other time that this gathering takes place. At Mass, you are in union with the larger community. In prayer at home, the fullness of the sign cannot be experienced. Only here before the tabernacle can you know this special unity. Only here can you know this special peace.

Granted, you probably won't be swept into ecstasy. You bring to the church the trials of your life. Distractions will occur. More disturbing are the sins and failings that you carry in your baggage. Proximity to Christ's Real Presence is akin to placing your soul in the refiner's fire. That which is corrupt in you will be purified by the burning love of Christ present just a few feet away. Before peace can be achieved, purification must always take place. If a visit to the Blessed Sacrament makes you feel uncomfortable, it is not because you shouldn't be there. Rather, the power of Christ's love is making a straight path for the gift of peace.

Invoke that peace today in your church. You may have to take nearly heroic steps to find the time to claim the gift of the Real Presence. In this case, the end will justify the means. Sitting in that quiet church away from the commercial chaos of these last days, you will begin to know, to experience, yes, to feel the love of the living Lord. To experience that love is to know the peace that passes understanding.

> Before the golden door she sat and wept
> a thousand earth-bound tears.
>
> She came to plead her case before the Lord.
> Her quest: serenity.
>
> She brought the most unusual complaint:
> a heart too full of love.
>
> She sought a countervailing force to calm
> the wings that fluttered up.
>
> He gave to her the holy dove of peace.
> They fly together now.

Lord, living and present, lift me up to new life in you. Carry me on the wings of eagles to that holy place of peace, that tabernacle of love, your Sacred Heart. Let me rest in your bosom and rejoice in your mercy.   Amen.

FOURTH SUNDAY OF ADVENT

Upon arriving, the angel said to her: "Rejoice, O highly
favored daughter! The Lord is with you. Blessed are you among
women." She was deeply troubled by his words, and wondered
what his greeting meant. The angel went on to say to her:
"Do not fear, Mary. You have found favor with God. You shall
conceive and bear a son and give him the name Jesus"
(Lk 1:28-31).

The peace that passes understanding is this: confidence
that we are loved by God. That God loves the sinner far
surpasses our ability to understand. This kind of love is so
different from the way of the world. The world is very
selective in bestowing its gifts; it loves only those who are its
own. If you want the world to smile upon you, you must
smile first; you must earn the world's benediction. God's
love, given freely even to those who don't love him, confuses
the world, confronts the world with a reality beyond its
understanding.

The Blessed Virgin Mary has always confused the world.
Her calm acceptance of God's will confronts those of us who
are too much *of* the world with a contending reality, an
alternative soulstyle suffused with that gift of the Holy Spirit
known as piety. In this context, piety is an abiding confidence in God's love. It is that confidence shining from the
Virgin's eyes in the midst of the trial described in today's
Gospel. "Deeply troubled" by a mysterious word that
seemed to require the sacrifice of her vowed virginity, Mary
nevertheless bowed to God's will. She knew neither the why
nor the how of her role in the drama. She knew only that she
would continue on a higher plane her life-long commitment
to conform her will to that of the God of Abraham, Isaac,
and Jacob. In following this vocation, she had gladly joined

the remnant of Jews who prepared every day for the coming of the Messiah. In this she set herself apart from the world, seeking from it no favors, investing in it no trust.

The Blessed Virgin Mary was ready to say, "Let it be done to me as you say" (Lk 1:38). By training and tradition she was the maid-servant of the Lord. Even though she was deeply troubled by the angel's words, she answered "Yes" to God's call because of the loving confidence she had in his saving mercy. This is the confidence you and I need to cultivate if we would know the peace that passes understanding. This kind of piety does not deny that the world exists nor does it shield us from pain. It seeks not to escape from the world but to test the world against the law of God. Mary was initially troubled by the angel's message because it did not conform to what she knew of the world. Her anxiety lasted only until she understood that it was God's will and God's reality.

Unless we have confidence in God's will, the season of Advent will be as bereft of peace as any other season can be. Since the world loves only its own, we are tempted to conform to secular reality in order to enjoy the blessings of the season. To thwart this temptation, to walk away from the materialism of this December requires a great deal of trust — trust that the Lord will walk with us, trust that he will lead us to a better place. This is precisely the confidence that the Blessed Virgin nurtured all her life to enable her to shape her will to that of God in the most disquieting situations.

Today, consider yourself part of that graced remnant in which Mary found the peace that passes understanding. Like her, you live in the world while continually testing it. In prayer, Scripture reading, and meditation, you hold up to the world the mirror of God's will. Those things in the world which produce a distorted reflection, you discard. Like

Mary, you are confident that God's way is the best way for you. Like Mary, you are meek and humble of heart, fully aware of the source of all blessing. You rest today in confidence and humility. You are glad to be apart as you live in the middle of humankind's turmoil. You have not separated yourself from the world; you have simply chosen to see it with God's eyes, to test it against the touchstone of his will.

God's reality is peace. Mary's story illustrates that God's peace does not take one out of the world. The Lord's path is through the world. His place of serenity is in the midst of the hubbub. We walk with him in confidence. We rest with him, trusting in his mercy and protection. Waves of anxiety may lap at our doorstep. A storm of pain may rattle the windows of our soul. The roar of commerce may deafen us. No matter to those who are confident in the Lord. We are at peace, for we have tested the world against his will and found the world wanting. What it wants is what we have: peace.

Do you trust the engineer
with arterial skill
not to place a deadman's curve
back behind that hill?

Can you rest assured in flight
twenty angels high
that the pilot really has
what it takes to fly?

Will you place your confidence
in the priestly vow
not to bruit your sins about
spilling why and how?

If upon these children of
    God you would rely,
    why this restless doubting when
    in his love you lie?

Lord God, source of all good things, I believe that you desire only the best for me. Strengthen my confidence in your loving mercy. Allow me to rest securely in your love and to meditate in serenity on your abundant blessings.   Amen.

DECEMBER 17th

Jacob was the father of Joseph
    the husband of Mary.
It was of her that Jesus who is called
    the Messiah was born.
Thus the total number of generations is:
    from Abraham to David,
        fourteen generations;
    from David to the Babylonian captivity,
        fourteen generations:
    from the Babylonian captivity to the Messiah,
        fourteen generations (Mt 1:16-17).

Many Americans have become fascinated by their roots. This near-obsession is fed by countless books and magazines on the subject of genealogy, enticing commercial offers to have designed one's very own coat of arms, and weekly newspaper columns tracing family names back through the history of a region. Searchers pore over dusty tomes in county courthouse basements. Hours and days spent on the quest for an ancestral vote of confidence add up to an inordinate amount of time consumed in rather egocentric research. To what purpose? To find something permanent in an ever-changing world. To be able to put a finger on a yellowed page and say, "See, here, I was in that man's loins. I had a verifiable beginning. I go back to a rock-solid place where I, at least in potential, was important." Finding one's roots makes a person feel less of a cypher in a faceless, constantly moving society.

This was the motive of the author of the Gospel according to Matthew. From the very beginning of his work, he wanted to prove to those Jews who became Christians after the resurrection that Jesus was the long-awaited Messiah. He gave Jesus roots. His scheme, with its forty-two generations so neatly divided into three equal parts, is a bit too neat to convince the modern reader of a valid generational procession. That wasn't the author's aim. He set out to illustrate Jesus' spiritual right to possess the title of "Anointed One." The Jewish leaders had rejected their true Savior, they had ostracized his followers, they had branded them as rootless disciples of a man without a past. This first section of Matthew's Gospel was written to prove not only that Jesus had a history, but more, that he had a noble lineage, and even more, that he was God's representative on earth. This argument was made with little regard for what today's genealogists would consider the scientific method. Rather, the author of the Gospel proved his religious thesis by revealing Jesus to be present in the loins of Abraham, David, and the patriarchs and kings of Israel. All of them were forerunners of Jesus Christ, the long-desired Messiah.

Today, put yourself in the place of the first Jewish Christians, those upstarts who were willing to sever their ties with home, family, and synagogue in pursuit of the truth. Picture them hearing the stories of the Apostles who left boat and father to follow Jesus. These stories were told to strengthen the new exiles, to assure them that, when Jesus put those who kept his word over her who gave him birth, he was telling the men and women of Matthew's community that their only family would be himself, their only home, his kingdom. In imitation of their Master, his followers would be on pilgrimage the rest of their earthly lives. Jesus began his life on the road. The Christmas story is a tale of two cities with the holy family somewhere in between. The Babe's first worshipers are shepherds who follow their flocks. The wise men are far from their homelands. The family continues its journey into Egyptian exile. The Son of Man has nowhere to lay his head.

Much of the turmoil in which we live occurs because so many in our society are spiritually rootless. Part of the genealogical phenomenon arises from a yearning to believe in something, if only the dim existence of a prominent forebear. Doubting their spiritual lineage, confused by the babble of contending truths even within their churches, our contemporaries begin to float with the current toward the whirlpool of indifference. This is far from the divinely directed pilgrimage of our spiritual ancestors; this is "going-with-the-flow" of the world.

Think of that ancient pilgrimage. The first Jewish Christians were internal exiles, living in Israel but allowed no longer to be part of its cultic life. Their decision to follow the Way cost them dearly, yet it was as nothing compared to the communion they enjoyed with the Father, Son, and Spirit. You and I, sorely tempted by the instinct of self-preservation to bind ourselves to this too, too solid world, strive to resist this false security. We would rather wander rootless than become the adopted sons and daughters of Mammon. We rejoice in the truth that is Jesus, we are rooted in the faith which is the Father's gift, we repose in the love by which the Spirit traces out our heritage and makes us one

with God. The tranquility of this season is not proportionate
to the length of your pedigree. Famous forefathers cannot
impose serenity upon their descendants. Only One who is
living and active now has the power to offer you peace: Jesus
Christ, yesterday, today, and forever. Be rooted in him.

> A people on a pilgrimage
> have little time to dwell
> upon the days behind them.
> Today has sorrows of its own,
> tomorrow their *bête noire*
> beyond the trees might find them.
> They keep their eyes upon the now,
> avoid the marketplace
> and hope the world won't mind them.
>
> What draws us on is soft beneath
> the babble of the crowd.
> O, how our ears revere it.
> A living voice, a word of peace:
> to listen is to burn
> with longing to come near it.
> Until one day, this day perhaps,
> the voice becomes a man
> for us to see and hear it.

*Father of the human family, you sent your Son to be the first-born of
many brothers and sisters. From you we trace our creation. In him
we find our re-creation. May his Holy Spirit guide us to your New
Creation. Amen.*

DECEMBER 18th

Joseph, her husband, an upright man unwilling to expose her
to the law, decided to divorce her quietly. Such was his intention
when suddenly the angel of the Lord appeared in a dream and
said to him: "Joseph, son of David, have no fear about taking
Mary as your wife. It is by the Holy Spirit that she has conceived
this child" (Mt 1:19-20).

"Saint Joseph Was A Just Man," as the hymn says. Indeed, he was a man who loved the law of Moses and fulfilled
it with zeal. When his betrothed was found to be with child,
he decided that he should not be the legally recognized
father because they had not yet come together. The law said
their engagement could be broken with the public exposure
of Mary's supposed adultery; failing that, a private declara-
tion in front of witnesses would do. In any case, this "divorce" could not be kept quiet forever. Joseph, the just man,
knew that his obedience to God's law would eventually bring
all involved to heartbreak.

You and I learn the same lesson nearly every day of our
Christian lives. To be a just man or woman, to be an obedient servant of God at work means inviting ridicule when
we turn down the offer to look at the degrading magazine or
to hear the salacious story. At home, it means incurring the
wrath of our children when we forbid them unwholesome
friends or entertainment. At school, it means getting the
honest "C" rather than the dishonest "A." Since St. Joseph
wasn't as cynical as our contemporaries, he probably missed
the chance to nod in jaded agreement with the statement,
"No good deed goes unpunished." That's the way it seems
sometimes. Constant striving to do good in the face of such
unrewarding prospects leads to moral exhaustion. We need

help to be moral in a frequently amoral and sometimes immoral world.

That help is ours in the gift of the Holy Spirit called fortitude. Another of our pre-Christmas presents, fortitude strengthens our souls for doing good while facing what seem to be unrewarding prospects. We see the effects of this gift in today's Gospel. It would seem that Joseph manifested a good deal of fortitude in refraining from making a public spectacle of what he assumed to be Mary's plight. As it turned out, he would be asked to be even stronger. In a dream, he learned the full extent of God's will in this situation. Rather than an affirmation of his discretion, Joseph heard a call to heroism. He was to go on as if nothing had happened, as if Mary were not pregnant. And when it became obvious to all that she was with child, he was to play the role of the proud poppa and give the baby a name, thereby exercising the right of legal paternity. This was enough to make even the most just of men search for an escape. Joseph, however, imbued with the charism of fortitude, saw God's will in this call. With courage born of faith in the divine plan, Joseph took Mary into his house and became, in fact, the foster-father of the Messiah, and, in appearance, the natural father of Jesus of Nazareth.

The gift of fortitude has been welcomed by women and men in every age; it seems an absolute necessity for Christian life today. The difficulties which confront the just are so varied and so subtle that merely human defenses cannot possibly measure up. Unless the Holy Spirit goes with us into the fray, we go practically unarmed. The season of Advent is a case in point. The most callow youth knows how to make parents feel guilty for not providing a cornucopia of presents. Mothers and fathers run themselves ragged to prevent filial disappointment under the Christmas tree. Instead, they should rely on their good sense that a gift is only a sign of love, not love itself. Such a stance takes fortitude. Workers of every description and level of organization over-indulge at office parties. In their stupor, their moral standards are forgotten with disastrous results. Moderation during the holidays calls for fortitude. At home, at work, at school, the secular trappings of commercial Christmas stifle the desire to prepare for the birth of the Prince of Peace. To speak up for the true meaning of the season in the face of so much materialism requires fortitude.

Fortitude can be bold-faced and ubiquitous as in the days of the martyrs of the early church. Or it can be hidden and subtle, evoked in the interface between private good and private evil. We see this secret strength in the series of just decisions which St. Joseph made. We need to experi-ence more of this interior endurance in our own lives when our difficulties are more subtle and our adversaries more cunning. To be at peace in the Lord and with ourselves, we must be confident that our will is his will. He offers this assurance to all who call upon him in time of trouble: The obstacles to good which you face today, and those beyond imagination which threaten your progress tomorrow, will be conquered not by your strength but by the power of the Holy Spirit, the gift of fortitude. With this assurance, cour-age drives out fear and serenity supplants anxiety.

Joseph, son of David, have no fear.
Shape your mind according to my will.
There is more to justice than you think,
more than simply legal rote and drill.

I am justice with a heart and soul.
Solace and compassion tip my scale.
Fortitude, my son! You must endure
while your rigid judgments fray and fail.

When your law lies shredded at your feet,
jots and tittles floating in the air,
form your choices round my words of love.
Temper right with mercy mild and fair.

Just and merciful Father, let the letter of the law not blind us to its spirit. Give us the strength and patience to endure the process of compassionate judgment. May we, with Jesus, the Sun of Justice always incline toward mercy.   Amen.

DECEMBER 19th

Zechariah said to the angel: "How am I to know this? I am an old man; my wife too is advanced in age."

The angel replied: "I am Gabriel, who stand in attendance before God. I was sent to speak to you and bring you this good news. But now you will be mute — unable to speak — until the day when these things take place, because you have not trusted my words. They will all come true in due season" (Lk 1:18-20).

"Christmas is for children" is a cliche shadowed by sadness for it is often used to rationalize neglect of the elderly at this time of year. In order not to deprive the kids of each and every sensation which December offers, parents are apt to deprive their own parents of the bare necessities of presence and communication. Unless they have earned, by their willingness to exhaust themselves in shallow holiday projects, the condescending epithets of "spry" and "chipper," grandparents are shunted aside like rusty boxcars on a weed-covered siding, brought out only for big moments like "the meal" or "the unwrapping." Still, they have a chance, albeit grudgingly given, to be heard over the voices of the children. They have not yet merited Zechariah's punishment.

That punishment is reserved for the aged infirm who are not spry or chipper, those in the back bedroom who can't be brought out because they are incontinent, those in the nursing home contending with the effects of a stroke which would frighten the children. For them, "Christmas is for children" translates to "living is for others." To the bedridden and institution-bound, December is the cruelest month. Those who are accustomed to regular visits by family members note a slackening in enthusiasm and a marked infrequency. After all, shopping is hectic, and Momma's not going anyplace. There is so much to be done outside this little room. No one wants to stand in the way of the children's happiness.

Now, in this last week of Advent, it is about time to stand in the way of the children's happiness, if necessary, and bring some genuine cheer to the elderly, especially to those confined to their beds or their rooms or in institutions. It would be inappropriate in this meditation to list activities and schedules for such an endeavor. Love is all that is needed, love will light the way, love will make the time. The aim of any loving visit to the aged infirm is to lift the punishment of muteness. They must be allowed to talk; more than that, they must have the right to be heard. When you go to the nursing home or visit a homebound relative or neighbor, call forth speech. Engage that lonely man in real conversation on a subject which he has chosen. Prove by your attention that you value the opinions of this great-grandmother. Because the words of the aged are so often ignored, many family members assume that their relatives no longer speak. The truth is that they have much to say, but there is no one to listen with love.

The peace of this season is not to be found only in quiet meditation. Contemplation of the word of God and his wonders on earth must lead to action. Jesus went away by himself to pray; he returned refreshed and ready again to heal those who came to him out of their pain and confusion. Visiting the elderly infirm doesn't mean you will be squandering your hard-won gift of peace on them any more than Jesus wasted his blessing of peace upon the suffering. Peace is God's gift and, like love, it grows in the giving.

As you strive to make this season meaningful for an elderly family member or an institutionalized stranger, let old Zechariah be your patron saint. Like the senior you love or the aged stranger you haven't yet met, Zechariah became mute because he thought he was too old to play a significant role in God's plan. Many of the elderly are sinking slowly into speechlessness because no one pays their words any mind. You must take them seriously or they may never speak again. Particularly in these days before Christmas, you must remember who they are and where they are. The elderly do not forget who you are and what they gave up for you and what they did for the world. Neither will God forget. Each of us has a debt of love to pay to those who smoothed our way, whether they be members of our family or part of the people of God.

To those who are old, alone, and infirm, you and I seem godlike in our mobility and acuity. Indeed, we do share his power to save them from muteness. Zechariah spoke again when he saw that he was important to God's plan. His role was to ratify his newborn son's name. "He signaled for a writing tablet and wrote the words, 'His name is John.' At that moment his mouth was opened and his tongue loosed, and he began to speak in praise of God" (Lk 1:63-64). Share with those you visit in this season a most holy holiday gift: the gift of speech. Show them how important they are to your plan.

> There is always someone waiting
> past the curtain
> in the bed
> under covers
> toe to head
> waiting for the words she harbors
> to impinge on
> pliant ear
> proving import
> nestles here.
>
> Galaxies of verse and scansion
> whirl across her
> lonely mind,
> worlds of thought to
> be defined
> only by the heeding voice of
> one who listens
> to her rhyme,
> never looking
> at the time.

Prince of Peace, I ask your blessing not for myself alone but for those who need me. Let me offer the rich fruit of these meditations to those who have outlived the timely harvest. Only your peace can sustain them in their lonely trial. Only my witness will manifest your gift.   Amen.

DECEMBER 20th

Therefore the Lord himself will give you this sign: the
virgin shall be with child, and bear a son, and shall name him
Emmanuel (because "God is with us") (Is 7:14).

Lord. Savior. Son of Man. Son of God. Lamb of God.
Messiah. Christ. Each of the titles given to Jesus highlights a
particular aspect of his mission. Covering the spectrum
from just judge to suffering servant, he presented many
faces, preached many messages. The variety of names given
to Jesus has sometimes confused his followers over the
centuries. How could he be at the same time a dispenser of
justice and a messenger of mercy? Could the Prince of Peace
really have said that he came to bring division to the world?
(See Lk 12:51.) And what about blessing a fallen woman and
then cursing a fig tree? When it comes to naming Jesus, one
title seems as good as another.

Or so it seems until one comes to today's first reading in
which Isaiah reveals Yahweh's name for the Messiah:
Emmanuel. This is the name which reconciles all of Jesus'
diverse titles. *Emmanuel* is the vine from which branch the
healing, the forgiveness, the power, and the suffering revealed by the various names of the carpenter's son. For while
each of the others adds to the richness of our understanding
of Jesus' mission and message, *Emmanuel* contains within its
divinely appointed syllables the essence of who Jesus is:
God-with-us.

This essential ministry of Jesus is never more deeply felt
than in your daily prayer. In your meditations, God is with
you. As you open yourself to the will of the Father, Emmanuel comes to sit beside you. He is the incarnate word of
God and he focusses his complete attention on you. Think
of it! God is with you, not in some perfunctory fulfillment of

an ancient promise, but intimately present to you, sharing whatever space you are ready to give him. He does not have a million things to do. You, at this moment, are his mission. You are his vocation. He is here for you; his attention never wavers, even when yours does. The prophecy of Isaiah takes flesh in your church or place of prayer. God is with you in the intimacy of your greatest friend, Jesus. Your soul fills his vision. He only has eyes for you.

How hard it is to believe that we are the center of God's dynamic attention. Often, we are distracted in our prayers because we think God is distracted. There are so many people in trouble, so many disasters impending that his attention couldn't be much more than that of an inspector in a sausage factory. As long as we aren't green and don't smell bad, he can concentrate on saving the world from itself. Not so. Emmanuel gives the lie to this surmise. Emmanuel says that God is *with* you NOW and *for* you NOW. *God-with-us* means God is with you in the intimate friendship of Jesus. Listen to Emmanuel today as he prays with you. Hear his words in yours. Only one whose knowledge of you comes from his deep, interior relationship with you can match your prayers word for word. Hear him praying beside you.

Emmanuel also means that your disappointment over the commercial frenzy of this season is a wise and godly re-action. God is with us as we strive to prepare for the holy day. God is with us as we take heroic measures to assure fifteen or twenty uninterrupted minutes of meditation. Of course, he is also with us when we are frazzled and exhausted from December's demands, but we don't know it. We don't really have a chance to taste the richness of his friendship until we let him lead us to our prayer place, until we soften our hearts hardened by hassles and feel the touch of his word. *Emmanuel* means God is tangible in the midst of chaos, present when we need him.

There can be only one explanation for the peace you have been able to salvage from these very busy days: Emmanuel. God has been with you at the center of the storm. Those days when you observed the frenetic pace of your family and friends with a certain air of detachment, those times when you were convinced that the whirl of the world could not catch you up, those moments were yours because Isaiah's prophecy had come true in your heart. You were sure that God was with you; the magnetic power of his serene simplicity drew you to him, pulled you from the maelstrom, clasped you in a peaceful embrace. Give thanks for those moments, then seek out once more the place, the time, the attitude, the insight that brought you to experience Emmanuel — the God who was always there.

> The poetry of love unbound
> > this brief encounter with the Lord
> > > which takes the measure of my heart
> > > ecstatic in its welcoming
> > > intense beyond my dream my death
> is traced upon this melting flesh.

> O sacred syllable of love
> > disturb the silent diffidence
> > > proclaim my need for him who speaks
> > > Emmanuel the godly word
> > > and sings in moments most serene
> of sweet communion in our world.

> This pent desire long since struck dumb
> > calls softly hoarsely in the still
> > > and waiting caverns of my hope
> > > that he is here to fill my want
> > > not now of logic but of love
> who bides with me and will again.

Word of God, let us imitate your love song in each moment of joy and sorrow. May those with whom we share this noisy planet listen when we fall silent, catch the rhythm of your benediction as we bless the world with good works, and, finally, join their voices with ours as we make your music and sing your peace.   Amen.

DECEMBER 21st

When Elizabeth heard Mary's greeting, the baby leapt in her womb. Elizabeth was filled with the Holy Spirit and cried out in a loud voice: "Blest are you among women and blest is the fruit of your womb" (Lk 1:41-42).

At the beginning of today's meditation, count slowly to twenty-two. From the time you start until the time you finish, another unborn child will be killed in the womb. Try counting the seconds now and see how this little exercise brings it home hard. One hundred thousand unborn murdered each month, 1,400,000 a year — these are mind-boggling, heart-searing numbers. The magnitude overwhelms us; since we can't get our experience around these figures, we tend not to dwell on them. But twenty-two seconds . . . that's something we can get hold of. Twenty-two seconds is a commercial on television, a time-check on the telephone, a traffic report on the radio. Twenty-two seconds is putting on your shoes and socks, making a bologna sandwich, microwaving a cup of coffee. Twenty-two seconds is putting the dog out, warming up the car, saying a Hail Mary. Twenty-two seconds is not statistical time or computer time but human time, time we can own and use. You can see twenty-two seconds on the watch on your wrist. That makes it your time. An unborn baby has just been killed on your time.

"Wait," you say. "This is four days before Christmas. Abortions are not going on today." If you believe that, try calling an abortion clinic in your town. You will be told to come in tomorrow, December 22nd. Call them on the 23rd if you want; they'll make an appointment for Christmas Eve. Many women have abortions before holidays to "get the thing out of the way." Since ninety-five percent of abortions are procured for the sake of convenience, and no one wants to carry an easily-solved problem into this festive season, abortion clinics do their best to please their customers even this close to Christmas. Who would deny a young mother's wish to be free of her burden in order to participate fully in the celebration of this joyous time?

John the Baptizer had been alive in his mother's womb for about six months when his mother's cousin, Mary, came to visit. John had fingers and toes in the right amount, legs, arms, genitals, ears, a nose and mouth — he had all the equipment necessary to make him not only a man but that man in history who was to be the immediate forerunner of the long-awaited Messiah. The only thing he didn't have at the moment of Mary's visit was the ability to efficiently sustain his own life. Unlike premature babies today who have the benefit of the latest in medical technology, John would have probably died rather quickly outside the womb.

Nobody wanted him to die, of course. He was a miracle baby, conceived out of time. His parents weren't just older than most parents, they "both were advanced in years" (Lk 1:7). More than that, Elizabeth was sterile; she had never given her husband a child. There was mystery surrounding the spark of new life that grew so urgently in Elizabeth's wrinkled womb. Now the mystery deepened when Mary arrived carrying her own child within her. Any other mother would have said her baby kicked; Elizabeth said, "The moment your greeting sounded in my ears, the baby stirred in my womb for joy" (Lk 1:44). Mystery had been awed by a greater mystery.

Could little John in his mother's womb have felt awe a month earlier? Could he have been affected by the proximity of the Son of God at four months, or three? Would the approach of the spark of life that illumines all life have brightened the mind of the unborn John at two months, or one? Wouldn't John have given a little tadpole wriggle at two weeks, or two days? The answer must be "Yes." The approach of the living pattern of all life must animate any individual life. As you and I are filled with grace and gratitude when we approach the sacraments, so must any life respond according to its nature at the approach of the one through whom that nature is bestowed. John leapt in the womb because the mediator of all life and his individual human life drew near.

In the twenty-two seconds between the last abortion and the next, there is still time to pray that the next mother will change her mind and allow another forerunner to come into the world, another herald of the Good News, who by lively words and joyful deeds will alert a little bit of the world to the approach of the Model of all life. Each newborn has the potential to become a modern John the Baptizer, a witness for Christ, another you, another me crying out to the people of God, if . . . if only the relentless cycle of death can be interrupted. You've been given twenty-two seconds to make a difference. You can make these moments your own in prayer. Minds can be changed by prayer. Pray for those contemplating abortion and for those assisting them. Pray that they will, perhaps for the first time in their lives, put their own convenience aside and think of a life that can leap within them. Pray also for the next baby in the womb of her or his mother as she reclines on the abortionist's table — the child who won't be saved, the one who will die for the sake of convenience. Beg God that the pain will be quickly over and the little one will mount swiftly to heaven, freed from the sharp blade of convenience. Pray for those who do and for those who don't. Pray for those who live and for those who won't. But hurry. You have only twenty-two seconds.

> The judgment of ten million souls
> broods dark upon the land:
> on mothers-once who cured themselves
> of urgent life's demand,
> on fathers-once who chose to shun
> responsibility,
> on justice-once transforming law
> to heartless anarchy.
>
> A nation of convenience,
> lethargic in its laze,
> consults the stars to find the joy
> it knew in former days:
> When will the laughter bubble up,
> when will our eyes grow bright?
> What is the shame that ushered in
> this long and cheerless night?
>
> The judgment of ten million souls
> destroys all hope for peace;
> true justice can't be realized
> until these murders cease.
> The jury of the Innocents
> deliberates each hour;
> in mute reproach they witness to
> the dying of our power.

Lord of life, gather into your heavenly home the millions of tiny innocents fatally forced from the womb. Lead those contemplating abortion away from tragedy. Rekindle in each of us a new respect for all human life.   Amen.

DECEMBER 22nd

God who is mighty has done great things for me,
    holy is his name;
His mercy is from age to age
    on those who fear him.
He has shown might with his arm;
    he has confounded the proud
        in their inmost thoughts.
He has deposed the mighty from their thrones
    and raised the lowly to high places (Lk 1:49-52).

To many Christians, even in our enlightened age, fear of the Lord means that God is making a list and checking it twice, gonna find out who's naughty and nice. If you're not nice, just as Santa Claus will leave a lump of coal in your stocking, so God will make you sit on a burning lump of coal for an eternity of punishment. This ghastly portrait of God is used to frighten people into obedience to rather questionable interpretations of the Ten Commandments and the laws of the Church. It works best when the Christian of any age remains a cowering child in his or her approach to a relationship with divinity.

Our last pre-Christmas gift of the Holy Spirit, fear of the Lord, always requires a disclaimer. *Fear* in this case does not refer to quaking and shaking in one's boots over the reckless caprices of a god who toys with humankind. *Fear* means *respect* for the might of a God who would wrap himself in weak flesh. It is the beginning of that special wisdom (See Si 1:12 and Ps 111:10) which calls the believer away from automatic obedience to the world's demands. Fear of the Lord might be called the gift of the silken cord because it gently draws our attention away from the gaudy extravagances of these last days before commercial Christmas and helps us to focus our prayer and meditations upon the essence of the holy day, that is, the realization that infinite power became incarnate in a stable where a cow could have stepped on him.

Fear of the Lord is the opposite of fear of importunate children, fear of uninvited guests, fear of unanswered greeting cards, or fear of unequal presents. This gift of the Spirit reminds us that offending the God who deigned to become man is far worse than disappointing children, guests, or friends. The latter may forgive us or they may not; we will survive either eventuality. But to survive without the forgiveness of God-with-us is an impossibility. Respect for God's person, his being, and his self-emptying love brings the truly wise man to his knees, the authentic seeker of peace to her prayer place. There, each respecter of majesty begins a private Magnificat weaving together praise and thanksgiving for warmly remembered blessings, petitions for present protection, and pledges of future obedience. As Mary, the model of self-effacement, offered the perfect Advent prayer, so each of us gives to God the promise of our fullest respect including our highest attention to his word, our most zealous pursuit of his kingdom, and our most constant offering of self. We can do no other, for in putting aside the mantle of majesty, he deserves all honor. In listening to his living word and in working for his accessible kingdom, we are in our self-offering wise beyond the world's measure.

Our Advent Magnificat is proof that we are on to the secret of this season. It may not be crystal-clear; frequently this mystery is difficult to make others understand, but we do possess it. The secret is this: God respects us! He respects us so much that he became one of us.

Fear of the Lord is our part in a mutual admiration society. God respects us far more than many of us respect ourselves. He has done great things for us. He has had mercy on us. He has raised us to high places. He has given us joy in knowing him. He has fed us, forgiven us, strengthened us. The quiet secret which the world with its tinsel and toys tries so hard to outshout is revealed in the humble prayer of a respectful virgin. As we pray our own Magnificat with our own memories and our own hopes, we strive to match her spiritual maturity. To be wise as Mary was is not to see God as an adversary to be appeased but as a giver of gifts to be accepted by those who believe in his generosity. Those who are poor in spirit have no other benefactor; they rely on God's mercy. This dependence, this certainty about God's compassion, this faith in his concern, in sum, this rock-solid assurance that God has infinite respect for us, is the final gift of the Holy Spirit.

The charism called fear of the Lord brings a serene perspective to the frenzy of these days, a peaceful release of all the strings you thought you had to pull to make sure everyone in your bit of the world had a happy holiday. Now, at rest in the knowledge of how valuable you are to God, you are certain that no one of worth will be unloved this Christmas. The Child of Bethlehem is given to all; thus, all are pearls of great price. Believe this, affirm it, live it. It is the beginning of wisdom.

Wisdom orders all to God,
charts the tranquil way.
Understanding purifies
hearts of vain display.
Counsel turns the dark to light
with right reason's ray.
Knowledge judges but by faith
what the nations say.
Fortitude empowers the soul
bravely to obey.
Piety looks up to God,
trusting, come what may.
Fear the Lord, cry all the saints,
put your pride away.
Seven gifts the Spirit sends,
blessing each new day.

Lord Jesus Christ, send your Spirit to rest upon us. Strengthen and enlighten your people in this age of competing philosophies and standards. May we hold to the right path as you lead us to the peaceful kingdom. Amen.

DECEMBER 23rd

Lo, I am sending my messenger
   to prepare the way before me;
And suddenly there will come to the temple
   the Lord you seek,
And the messenger of the covenant
   whom you desire.
Yes, he is coming, says the Lord of hosts (Ml 3:1).

The sleek Eurosedan was coming up fast behind me —
too fast, I thought, for conditions on this narrow road spat-
tered with patches of ice. He blinked his brights and swept
around my skittish little car. The swirl of light snow blinded
me for a moment, but not before I glimpsed the driver with
one hand on the steering wheel and the other holding a
telephone handset to his ear.

To catch my breath, I drove on the shoulder for a while,
crawling along, listening to the thin crust of ice crack under
my tires, wondering what important call the driver had
received as he put my life at risk, wondering if he had made
some kind of remark to corporate headquarters or his rac-
quetball partner. "Hah! I just blew a little guy off the road."
More likely, he never looked back.

Cellular car telephones, belt-on beepers, citizens' band
radios, automatic message recorders all express our modern
desire to be informed. We want to miss nothing of import.
Television news on a twenty-four hour basis keeps us up to
date with the latest tragedies and turmoil. To our eternal
glory, we will be known as the people who invented,
perfected, and then deified the "information industry." We
have made news in all its forms — personal, parochial,
national, galactic — into one of the ruling gods of our
pantheon. The great god *News* told the driver of the
Mercedes that my life meant less than his information fix.

Think today of the news you long to hear. What are the
messages which move you? A raise in salary. A larger office.
Higher standing in your community. The ideal lover. Suc-
cess in college. Obedient children. We blush to admit that
the kind of news that makes our ears tingle with pleasure has
a lot to do with our own good fortune. Even our Advent
prayer for peace is a plea that the calming word of the Lord
might be pronounced first in our own hearts, our home, our
community. We may disdain the information industry

with its technological toys, ephemeral celebrity, and manufactured news. We may find amusing those who wire themselves for instant messages and program their telephones with plaintive requests for vital statistics "after the sound of the tone." We share with those we judge as foolish, however, an inherent thirst for good news. The difference lies in the media chosen. They go to their recording machines and car telephones. We go to prayer.

We go to the right place. There is nothing wrong with wanting to hear good news if you realize that it will not come from NBC, CBS, or ABC. We were created to hear good news, but not on our C. B.'s, cellulars, or answering machines. As Christians, we stand on the shoulders of the Jews who themselves stood on tiptoe for centuries to hear the good news. Our first reading today is typical of God's various promises to our spiritual ancestors. Every prophet said it in a different way; each was blind to the fullness of its dimensions, but it boils down to this: "Have I got news for you! It's about a new covenant that cannot be broken, a new agreement between God and humankind that subsists in the God-man who will be your Savior. This new covenant will be tried in the fire of suffering, seem to be torn to pieces in the jaws of death, yet emerge to live as long as the God-man lives. And he will live forever!"

This is the only news we need seek. This is the only word that draws us to prayer. This is the only good fortune promised in this season or any season. This is the message of every prophet, the peal of every church bell, the rhyme of every hymn, the point of every sermon, the secret of every confession, the commitment in every vow, the peace in every promise. This is the Good News.

In your prayer today, don't say a word. Just listen for the Good News: Unbreakable covenant. God-man. Savior. Suffering and death. Triumph and eternity. If God would send a people into the desert with this news, rescue them from themselves again and again, draw from them messengers to keep fresh this news, conceive in them his only-begotten Son to be this news-made-man, heal him of death and command that the news of his triumph be proclaimed to all nations — if God, through the power of his Son's Spirit, would inspire millions of longing listeners over some two thousand years with this Good News, then you and I should be silent in prayer today. Let God do the talking. He speaks the Word-made-flesh.

I got an earful just the other day.
The lines were crossed somewhere along the way.
He spoke of doubt;
she of mistrust:
He couldn't see;
she was unjust . . .
until they both ran out of things to say.

Not so the newsman with his nightly spate
of horrors launched upon the world by fate.
There is no end
of drear reports
of lost attempts
and last resorts
which cast an endless pall upon man's state.

The journals of the day sketch out in ink
the portrait of a people at the brink.
The paper can
be dropped, but still
your hands retain
the stain until
you cleanse yourself of what the worldly think.

So come away from this cacophony
and train your ears to fathom mystery.
He whispers now,
the Prince of Peace;
his call endures
though worlds shall cease:
Abide with me as I abide with thee.

*Word of God, help us to hear your call in the weak voices of those we
choose not to listen to during this season: the poor, the elderly, the
homeless, the orphans. You came to the weak, were born among
them, and now stand with them pleading their cause. Help us to hear
you.   Amen.*

DECEMBER 24th

All this is the work of the kindness
of our God;
he, the Dayspring, shall
visit us in his mercy
To shine on those who sit in darkness
and in the shadow of death,
to guide our feet into the way
of peace (Lk 1:78-79).

They are coming. Soon they will arrive. Many have already begun the journey. The sandwiches are in the hamper
on the back seat. The kids have been warned about fighting.
The service stations and rest stops are marked in red.
Hearth or table or wreath on the front door is glorified in
the memory of each traveler. *Home.* Decades away, three
children, one in college, eight years in your third house, and

you still tell them you're coming *home*, that you will return once again to the source to plant kisses on proffered cheeks and place slim gifts under the tree and praise the cook and reprise the past. If you are one of these, the blessed whose roots have survived reckless fate, let your meditation this day be upon a fond tableau of hearth and table and wreath. Thank God for his benediction, his blessed protection upon you and yours. May peace precede you on your journey.

Many journey not on this insistent eve, but are forced to meander among memories. You have outlived family and friends. Home is where you are now. You made the attempt, hung a wreath, looped lights around the hedge. It's not the same as it used to be. Life lines have unravelled and many have played out. Although you too are fraying at the edges, you haven't reached the end of the line. The Star of Bethlehem that shone from the top of the family tree so long ago still gleams in your eyes. God's benediction upon you is the richness of memory.

Some set out in haste this day for gatherings unplanned. A lingering illness decides to close the play. The curtain will come down in a matter of hours. From ribbons and wrapping paper, you are plucked by death's messenger. A midnight plane, a fluorescent hospital, a vigil sung in groans instead of Glorias. The others arrive, each betraying a thimbleful of resentment over a rude truth: Life ends; some lives end on Christmas Eve. Your sustenance, your courage, your consolation this night is your faith — not a faith of creeds or formulas or lines of flowing prayer, but an inarticulate faith. You have few words for this birth-reversed vigil, this attendance upon death rather than life. God's benediction upon you is the serenity of surrender.

Some are quite unfree tonight, prevented from embracing by bonds of duty which limit movement. Gripping the squad car's wheel, your hands long to cup the dimpled chin.

The scalpel so delicately balanced in your fingers is not the burnished blade poised over the juicy bird. At switchboard, control panel, coffee counter, registration desk, monitor and microphone, hose rack, confessional screen, prisoners of good order are not so merry gentlemen and ladies. Time-and-a-half, three days off, a bonus check will but slightly assuage the pain of this vain vigil. The clock will fall well into Christmas Day before the watch is up. All are where they are supposed to be tonight; you are out of place and time. Only God is with you. His benediction is his affirming presence. You mean so much to him just where you are.

Some are pretending indifference tonight. You believed in God once, but you grew out of it. Teachers and preachers, ill luck, bad luck, no luck, meaningless pain, unanswered prayers helped you graduate to the floating agnosticism the world calls sophistication. The trouble is that every December 24th you rediscover what a child you really are. But whose child? So tonight you will meet feathered friends over too many drinks and discuss the charade of Christmas. God's benediction upon you? His Being. Whether you know it or not, whether you like it or not, his "is" makes you his child.

The Dayspring will visit us all this night; not just the light, but the source of all light will be protection for the traveler, memory for the old, peace for the anxious, presence for the laboring, being for the unbeliever. All those in darkness will turn to the radiance in the East and see illuminated before them the path to peace. Those in the shadow of death will lift their eyes to the Eastern Star and receive their benediction. Upon all of these will shine the kindness of our God in the smile of a little child.

slowly they creep to the cave
muzzling the lambs with their hands
lest bleat provoke wail
and fear destroy peace

sadly they trudge to the cave
bearing the oils in their hands
and weep for the peace
that death has destroyed

surely the women know death
can not be changed into life
but how moved the stone
and what is that gleam

softly at first glows the light
caught in a mother's embrace
then blots out the stars
in shepherds' wide eyes

subtly these eves are alike
both bringing hope to the night
each morn heralds life
the Son raised from sleep

Father in heaven, with you and with the world, we keep vigil tonight. Your people wait in hope for the promised Prince of Peace. Let us know his coming. We long to welcome him into our hearts.   Amen.

CHRISTMAS DAY

The angel said to them: "You have nothing to fear! I come
to proclaim good news to you — tidings of great joy to be
shared by the whole people. This day in David's city a savior
has been born to you, the Messiah and Lord. Let this be
a sign to you: in a manger you will find an infant wrapped in
swaddling clothes." Suddenly, there was with the angel a
multitude of the heavenly host, praising God and saying,
   "Glory to God in high heaven,
      peace on earth to those on
         whom his favor rests" (Lk 2:10-14).

The new day has come, the day of the Christ, Christ's
day, Christ's Mass. Christmas is an affair of the heart. Not all
dreams come true today, but hope is born anew in the heart
of each child of God. This day of grace turns through the
hours, a kaleidoscope of joyous surprise, misty remembrance, and shy gratitude. Christmas is a little child born in
our memory. Christmas is a majestic king come to rule over
his people. Christmas is the groaning board and the groaning diners. Christmas is a blizzard of torn wrapping paper.
Christmas is the straining choir and the straw under the
altar. But, above all, Christmas is Judgment Day.

"All rise," orders the bailiff. All eyes are upon the judge
as he strides from his chambers. His face is solemn, betraying no emotion, yet there is a certain kindliness about his
eyes. He sits, straightens his robes, and prepares to read the
verdict. In their anxiety, those packing the courtroom remain standing, now rising as one on tiptoe in anticipation of
the decision. Every man and woman in this courtroom is a
defendant.

"I find each defendant," intones the judge, "favored. I
find every defendant worthy. I find all who stand before me

in such trepidation valuable, worthwhile, estimable, of infinite potential. I find all of you lovable. My judgment upon you is love, and as proof of my love I give you my love-made-flesh, my only-begotten Son."

Christmas is Judgment Day. Since the First Sunday of Advent, we have been preparing to hear the verdict, hoping that it would be Good News. We have fought the world for space and time to listen for the Lord. Amid the jangle of cash registers and the prattle of pitchmen, we have strained to catch the affirming word, that tantalizing pronouncement of our dignity. And now the judgment has been handed down, come to life in a manger. The Christ-child is God's enfleshed approval of our humanity. That delicate sheath of skin on the tiny arm is our skin. That fast-pumping heart beats with ours. Those wondering eyes fix upon our world. Christmas is the day when we learn that God cared so much for us that he sent his very best; he became one of us.

Now, as the judge smiles, one last item remains on the docket. The former defendants are silently embracing. Their wonder at this revelation, their burden of gratitude has rendered them speechless; they have no trouble hearing the final words. "Because you have been found favored, valuable, worthy, and lovable, I sentence you to . . . peace." The judge rises and removes his outer robes revealing the purple of majesty. Instead of returning to his chambers, he steps forward into the throng, his princely visage alight with love and understanding. On each forehead he bestows a benediction while the people press upon him, their tongues loosed in welcome. "Wonder-Counselor," they cry. "God-Hero, Father-Forever," they sing. "Prince of Peace," they pray.

It is too much for any of the earthbound, too much for you and me this day. Creator, Savior, Spirit abides with us, touches us with love: just a tiny spark of life but enough to push back the curtain of darkness to reveal the radical dignity given us in his coming. Our poor senses strain to contain the touch of his love. Our minds labor to perceive that upon which reason founders. Finally, after weeks of waiting and hoping and praying, insight comes with the sweet release of tears: judgment walks among us, affirms our being, approves our struggle, blesses our destiny. Our senses give way, our minds give in, our very souls cannot contain this immense consolation. We submit to love-among-us, love-made-flesh, love-become-us, and in this serene submission, tears of happiness and wonder wash from our faces all trace of constriction, restraint, and anxiety; tears of recognition and gratitude cleanse our vision of all that would blind us to the One who is God's judgment upon us. At one and the same time we see him wrapped in swaddling clothes, wearing the teacher's seamless garment, bound in the winding cloth, and radiant in the robe of resurrection. We catch at the purple hem of majesty in our midst and, weeping for joy, cling to our princely brother. Christ's day is here, the day of our judgment. Mercy mild embraces every child of God. The verdict is a kiss of peace.

How perfectly angelic was
the song the shepherds heard,
this guileless hymn of praise for God
who made himself absurd
by leaving in his plunge the pure
and selfless spirits for
rebellious children wrestling on
creation's littered floor.

Of glory, peace, and favor sang
the choir from heav'n above
while far below the great unwashed
beheld God's gift of love.
The angels were not judged that morn,
beyond reproach they flew,
no part of this exchange by which
mankind was born anew.

The earthbound then were lifted up
to touch the holy face,
to glimpse the blest potential of
each member of their race.
Rejoicing in the chance to share
divinity on high,
they laughed while simple spirits cried
to God who passed them by.

Father of heaven and earth, by sending us your Son as proof of your love and our worth, you have given us the opportunity to share in your divinity as you have shared in our humanity. May this holy exchange be the heart of our Christmas celebration. We make this prayer in the name of the Prince of Peace, your Son and our brother, Jesus, the Christ.   Amen.

A FINAL WORD

The Hebrew word for peace, *shalom*, stands for more than the absence of anxiety. In the Old Testament, *shalom* means wholeness, a felicitous blending of health, harmony, and prosperity. When we ask God for the gift of *shalom*, he sends us his Son to restore our well-being, to reconcile us with his Father and with our brothers and sisters, to make our world whole again. Is there a better word for this reintegration of our lives and our world than "salvation"? Thus, peace is our salvation.

In our quest for peace during this Advent season, we have sought the restoration of personal and social harmony in Christ Jesus. By praying for the saving grace which is ours in the gifts of the Holy Spirit, we have expressed our longing to be made whole in our personal lives and to become one with those who suffer, to join our desire to the hopes of those who yearn to experience the touch of the Prince of Peace. For us and for them, peace is *shalom*, the tranquil balance of now and not yet. Peace means reconciliation with God, the restoration of humanity's rightful relationship with its Creator. Peace means that deep, inner confidence born of a month of prayerful preparation, the certainty that Christ had inspected our premises, found them suitable, and accepted the invitation to come and dwell in our hearts.

Now, the candles sputter out, the ruddy faces depart, the last carol is sung. Now, the holy day ends and with it the zeal of Advent. Now, the sky is gray again and the sharp wind makes us shiver despite the wine and the embracing. The calendar brings us up short. Winter is only three days old.

Three long months stand stamping their feet in the cold. Now, peace must prove its mettle.

We seldom think of peace as strength, but strong it must be to carry us through the chill reality of winter. Only those who cradle within themselves the balanced power of *shalom* can gaze comfortably into the pale eye of the future. The measured preparation of Advent will be tested as each of us is called upon to share our gifts with winter's refugees. They will beg from us reconciliation and restoration. They will listen to our voices to hear Good News. They will seek salvation in our saving deeds. They will turn to you and me who have spent a month together with the Prince of Peace learning his benediction and watching his smile. They will come to us with arms outstretched to receive all we have seen and heart. It is all that we have, but more than enough: that smiling benediction called peace.

But now in Christ Jesus you who once were far off have been brought near through the blood of Christ. It is he who is our peace, and who made the two of us one by breaking down the barrier of hostility that kept us apart. In his own flesh he abolished the law with its commands and precepts, to create in himself one new man from us who had been two and to make peace, reconciling both of us to God in one body through his cross, which put that enmity to death. He came and "announced the good news of peace to you who were far off, and to those who were near"; through him we both have access in one Spirit to the Father (Ep 2:13-18).

May you know God's shalom, *Jesus Christ, who comes to make you whole once more. May you experience the harmony which the Holy Spirit brings to all human relationships. May you bless the troubled and trembling refugees of winter with the warmth of love. In the* not yet *of this yearning world, may you be peace* now.